MW01484087

Church Words
origins and meanings

Stephen E. Moore

Forward Movement Publications
Cincinnati, Ohio

© 1996
Forward Movement Publications
412 Sycamore Street, Cincinnati, Ohio 45202

ISBN 0-88028-172-3

The following essays were originally published as bulletin inserts, "sound bites," to help inform members of the congregations where they were used. In the spirit in which they were written, individual articles from this book may be quoted in parish educational materials, provided that the materials are not for sale and that the following attribution is made: "Reprinted from *Church Words,* by Stephen E. Moore, published by Forward Movement Publications, 412 Sycamore Street, Cincinnati, OH 45202 USA."

—

Stephen E. Moore lives near Seattle where he serves part time as a priest and part time as a judge. He also teaches ethics and moral theology in the Episcopal Diocese of Olympia's Diocesan School of Theology.

Contents

Architecture

Sanctuary

Chancel

Nave

Narthex

Sacristy

Spire/Steeple

SANCTUARY _____

In churches built on the western pattern, the sanctuary is at the head or east end of the structure. In the Old Testament the holy place where God was present was called the sanctuary. While the Hebrews were in the desert, this meant the Tent of the Presence (Exodus 35-40); in the time of King Solomon, this meant the Temple in Jerusalem (1 Kings 6-7). There are a great many parallels which can be drawn between catholic Christian sanctuaries and their Hebrew counterparts.

The more Eucharist-centered the denomination, the greater the importance of the sanctuary. Most sanctuaries are located several steps above the main-floor level of the nave. This increases their visual prominence and affords a better view of what occurs there.

The altar is the focal point of the sanctuary and usually nothing is located therein which detracts from its centrality. While there was a time when sanctuaries were crowded with objects of veneration (statues, paintings), the modern trend is away from this practice. A properly designed sanctuary affords room for an ambry, a credence table and seating for the ministers of the table.

The presence of God in the Jewish sanctuary was symbolized by a fire kept burning at all times. A candle or lamp burns over or near the altar in those churches where the sacrament is reserved in the sanctuary signaling a holy Presence.

Rules in ancient Judaism permitted only the priests to enter the tent or the inner Temple; only the High Priest could approach the Holy of Holies at its center. In the Eastern Church, that part of the church located inside and behind the screen called the iconostasis is called the sanctuary. Many Eastern churches prohibit women from going into this area. The Western Church has treated the sanctuary as "holy ground" in its tradition and ordinarily only the ordained (and those almost as "holy," e.g. acolytes and altar guild) have entered. These rules are slowly fading as social barriers to women and ecclesiastical barriers to lay people fall.

The writer of Hebrews compared the work of the High Priest in the sanctuary to the work of Jesus Christ (chapters 8-9). Holy Scripture has also presented the individual Christian as a sort of sanctuary made holy by the indwelling of the Holy Spirit. The sanctuary in Christian churches remains a lively symbol of the presence of God in our midst, particularly in the Holy Eucharist.

CHANCEL

In many churches built on a classic Western pattern, there is an area between the sanctuary, where the altar is located, and the nave, where the faithful are seated. This area is often set apart from the nave in several ways. The floor may be a step higher than that in the nave (and the sanctuary a step higher than this floor). This area may be set off from the nave by a rail, screen, or fence, still seen in some older English and American churches. It is from this rail that the area derives the name "chancel," from the Latin "cancelli" meaning railing or lattice.

Another usage of the term chancel is to describe wherever the choir is seated. This is an incomplete understanding of the term. Some choirs are "flown" with the organ in a gallery at the back of the church, and this gallery is in no sense a chancel. The common location for the choir is in the chancel in the front of the church between the people and the altar. This is also the proper location for the vested ministers during the Daily Office and the Liturgy of the Word in the Holy Eucharist.

In the past, entrance to the chancel was limited to clergy and to those lay people who had a role there—acolytes, lectors, lay readers and choir—who were vested like clergy when they entered. An exception to this practice in the Church of England occurred during that period when infrequent communion was the norm. The invitation "draw near with faith" was responded to only by those who intended to receive Holy Communion, moving from the nave up to the chancel. This practice continued into the 19th century.

Many older chancels contain "stalls"—seats and prayer desks set apart by low fences or railings from each other, sometimes with a door or gate by which they are entered. As a rule, these stalls face toward the main aisle running from the nave to the sanctuary, rather than toward the altar. The stalls are sometimes denominated by their intended occupant: clergy (for leading the Daily Office), preacher's, deacon's, curate's, cantor's and even one specially for the "ruler of the choir" from which the master may keep an eye on the small boys in his charge.

The modern chancel is more flexible than its predecessor. It is the location of numerous activities—for example, "chancel drama" in which the Gospel is acted out, rather than simply read aloud to the congregation.

NAVE

The central part of a church, where the faithful stand or sit during divine service, is called the nave. The name derives from the Latin "navis" which means "ship." This is possibly because one of the ancient symbols for the church was a ship. Other areas are set apart for the choir, the ministers of the word and the ministers of the table.

Christian assemblies in pre-Christian Rome likely took place in private homes. The triclinium (dining hall) of a patrician Roman home would have suited nicely both the liturgies of the word and the table. Some assemblies may also have been held in an atrium which was a sort of courtyard in the center of a home.

After Constantine's Edict of Milan in 313, Christian churches were built in the Roman Empire after the pattern of the Roman law courts. The Roman hall of justice was called a basilica, hence the basilica-style of church. The judge's chair became the bishop's throne; the two pulpits for the two lawyers became the places from which were read the Gospel and the other lessons.

Naves tended to be oblong and oriented toward the east. This was not the only shape of naves, however. Round churches are not, as might be imagined, strictly modern. Charlemagne had one built at Aix-la-Chapelle between 796 and 804.

By the 11th century, the classic patterns of church structure had been settled. The medieval church was divided into distinct parts: (1) the sanctuary, where the high altar was located, (2) the chancel or choir, where the choristers were situated, (3) the nave, where the congregation gathered, and (4) the transept, where side altars or chapels were located, completing a cruciform shape for the church. Medieval cathedrals are known for their extreme longitudinality, Gothic cathedrals for their extreme verticality.

With the rise in importance of preaching beginning in the 16th century came a shift toward providing seating (of which there had previously been little), establishing a line of sight between parishioners and pulpit, and an increased concern for audibility.

The Eastern Church has largely maintained what the Western Church lost by installing seating in the nave. Eastern liturgy is done on the feet or on the knees; only the elderly and infirm sit. The western practice of sitting in rows increases passivity and is best suited to receiving instruction or watching a spectacle.

Modern naves in novel (and sometimes shocking) shapes attempt to overcome this passivity, in order to restore the liturgy as the work of the people.

NARTHEX

In Classical Greek, the word narthex meant a large funnel. As the Greek language expanded over time, narthex came to mean a porch or portico, presumably because people "funneled through it" to gain entry to a building.

In early Christian churches, a narthex was a porch located at the west end of the building where penitents and catechumens (those not yet admitted to the Holy Eucharist) gathered. Over time, the narthex came to be any vestibule opening into a nave.

The use of the term derives from the Eastern Church. Churches built on the Orthodox pattern also had an outside porch called the exo-narthex, which was an extension of the narthex.

In the Western Church, narthexes which began as porches became rooms as it was found necessary to enclose them because of the many liturgical functions which occurred there.

In medieval times, the church narthex served various community functions. Banns of marriage were posted there, as were other legal notices. Some minor courts conducted legal business on the porches of churches.

In churches built on Western traditional lines, the narthex is a practical place, serving as an entry hall and often equipped with cloak racks and umbrella stands. Such a classic Western narthex is equipped with two sets of doors: one opening to the exterior of the church and the other leading into the nave. The doors between the narthex and the nave are customarily quite tall, affording room for a mitered bishop or an acolyte carrying a cross to pass through with ease. Traditional furnishings include a holy water stoup, a box to collect offerings for the relief of the poor, and a reader board on which the times of services are posted.

In some modern churches, the baptismal font is located within the narthex. The symbolism of such a location is that, just as the narthex is the entry into the church building, so Holy Baptism is the entry into the mystical Body of Christ which is the Church.

The narthex in the parish church is liturgically important at the Great Vigil of Easter when the new fire is struck there and used to light the Paschal Candle. The narthex of a cathedral becomes liturgically important at the enthronement of a newly-consecrated bishop, who begins the service by knocking on the inner doors to gain admission to the church.

SACRISTY

A sacristy is a most prosaic place. It exists as a place (or places) where sacred vessels are maintained and stored, where the vestments and hangings are kept, and from which the housekeeping of the worship areas of the church is conducted. It is often a room near the sanctuary; some churches have only one; others as many as three or four.

To serve the church well as a place of storage, the sacristy must be cleverly designed to accommodate the size and shape of many odd items which must be kept and protected. In addition to normal vessels, such as chalice and paten, vases and altar linens, there are many items which are used only occasionally—figures for the Christmas creche, Advent wreath, funeral palls—which must be kept as well. In addition to the many shelves, drawers and cupboards in a typical sacristy, some are equipped with a safe or locked cupboard in which the most valuable items are kept.

As the center of church housekeeping, some sacristies contain broom closets, ironing boards, utility sinks and storage space for cleaning agents. The ideal sacristy has two sinks: a utility sink and a piscina. The utility sink must be large enough to wash the large objects. Another sink, called a piscina, drains directly onto the earth and is used exclusively to rinse the vessels which have contained consecrated wine or the water of baptism.

In some smaller churches, vestments are kept in the sacristy and the ministers dress there. Where a separate room is provided for storing and donning vestments, it is properly called a vestry. Very large churches may have multiple vestries for clergy, choir, and acolytes. A vestry properly contains closets and drawers in which the vestments (and sometimes the hangings) are kept, a small table on which the celebrant's vestments are laid out by a member of the altar guild, a full-length mirror and a shelf for books to be used in the service. A small sink is sometimes provided where the ministers may wash their hands before vesting.

Various short forms of prayer are sometimes posted in the vestry—prayers to be said while putting on vestments, a form for blessing holy water, a thanksgiving after the Holy Eucharist.

Ancient sacristies have been found in the ruins of 5th century churches in Syria. Medieval cathedrals provided sacristies behind the apse and on either side of the sanctuary. The ideal situation of a modern sacristy is the same: adjacent to the sanctuary, with access to the sanctuary by one door and to the outside or the rest of the church building through another.

SPIRE/STEEPLE

Atop many churches in Europe and the United States, towers are completed with a pyramidal or conical structure tapering to a point aimed at heaven.

A steeple is any tower-like structure arising from the top of a church or other building. A spire is an ornamental culmination of a tower or steeple, rising still higher into the sky.

"Spire" is a noun derived from the Middle English "spir" which is related to the Old Norse noun "spira" and thus probably entered the English language during the Viking raids and occupations. It first meant the sprout or spike of a plant, narrow and reaching up, but came to mean the pointed structure on top of a building. "Spire" has been incorrectly identified as deriving from the Latin "spiritus" meaning breath or life or spirit.

In English churches, spires typically mount towers, as in the well-known spire of Norwich Cathedral in Norfolk, which is actually one large spire surrounded by four smaller similar spires, each at one of the corners of the tower.

Such structural ornaments originated in the 12th century and evolved toward taller, slimmer forms. The building of towers grew in popularity as the art of bell-ringing ascended. Bell towers are a standard feature of English churches since the 14th century. The major cities of Europe competed to erect the tallest spires to top their cathedrals and other major churches. This competition often resulted in poorly designed and poorly erected spires which toppled in a relatively short time. The spire of Salisbury Cathedral, not part of the original plan of the building, rises 404 feet over the transept and is supported by arches added after the nave was built in order to support the additional weight.

By the 17th century, spires were integral to ecclesiastical architecture in Germany, France and England. Christopher Wren's 17th century English church designs typically include relatively simple spires. In 18th century Austria, an edict of toleration was issued which permitted Lutherans, Calvinists and Greek Orthodox to conduct worship in buildings so long as the buildings did not have steeples. This prevented non-Roman Catholic church buildings from being confused with Roman Catholic churches which, presumably, all had steeples.

Nineteenth century American churches feature all manner of spires, particularly those designed during the Gothic Revival (1840-70).

Furnishings

Altar

Pulpit

Lectern

Credence Table

Altar Rail

Baptismal Font

Pews

Kneeler

Cathedra

ALTAR

The first celebrations of the Holy Eucharist were probably done around wooden tables in the homes of early Christians. The reference in Hebrews 13:10 to "our altar" may or may not refer to the eucharistic table. The word "altar" comes from the Latin word "altare" which means high or elevated. This word was used by many of the early Fathers (Ignatius, Cyprian and Tertullian) to describe the table on which the Eucharist was celebrated.

Stone altars rapidly became the norm in Christian worship. This may have arisen from the practice of celebrating the Eucharist on the tombs of martyrs in the Catacombs. This is also the likely source of the Roman Catholic practice of enclosing the relics of martyrs in stone altars, which practice continues today.

During the Reformation, the use of stone altars was associated with the Roman doctrine of the repetitive sacrifice of the mass and therefore many reformed churches replaced the altar with a simple table. The American Book of Common Prayer speaks interchangeably of the table, the Holy Table and the altar.

Altars are traditionally made of stone. If the entire altar cannot be made of stone, the surface (called the mensa) is often stone. The mensa is normally inscribed with five Greek crosses—one in each corner and one in the center—symbolic of the five wounds of Christ.

The oldest altars were free-standing and the celebrant likely stood behind them facing the people. Medieval altars were built against the east wall. Modern altars have returned to the original location and the celebrant to a posture facing the congregation. Wherever placed, the altar must be the focal center of the church.

Ancient churches had only one altar. The

construction of multiple altars in a single church arose from the Roman Catholic practice of celebrating multiple daily masses. This was never an English custom.

The altar is normally covered with two cloths: the frontal, which is an ornate hanging across the front of the altar, and the altar cloth, which is a long white cloth placed over the top of the altar, hanging down over both ends. The American Episcopal Church's Book of Common Prayer (BCP) requires only a clean white cloth spread on the altar (p. 406).

The special nature of the altar is reflected by the rule that it must be blessed by a bishop prior to its use. (BCP p. 577) Sometimes the celebrant kisses the altar or incenses it before beginning the eucharistic prayer. While the altar is not a carved idol to be worshiped, it does stand as a sign of the presence of God in the Holy Eucharist and should be venerated accordingly.

PULPIT

In the early Christian Church, the bishop preached from where he sat. The development of a stand-up preaching place is "modern" in the sense that it began in the 12th or 13th century and became generally accepted in the Late Middle Ages. The preaching stand is called a pulpit from the Latin "pulpitum" meaning a scaffold, stage or stand. The canons of 1604 required that a pulpit be provided in every English church and that it be "comely and decent" as well as "seemly kept."

A pulpit is normally constructed of either wood or stone, in keeping with the decor of the interior of the church. They are often fashioned with a gate which can be closed (to prevent the preacher from pitching over backwards) leading to stairs or steps by which the pulpit is mounted. The English ceremonialist Percy Dearmer also suggests that the pulpit should be surrounded with a rail because "Englishmen . . . find their hands rather in the way" and they will "avoid fingering their garments" if there is a rail to grasp.

Pulpits grew in elaboration and decoration, particularly from the 16th century. They may be adorned with illustrations deriving from their use: God giving the Law to Moses, Jesus preaching, the symbols of the four Evangelists. Outstanding examples of ornate pulpits are found in the carved wooden pulpits of the Netherlands and the sculpted marble pulpits of Italy. The front of the pulpit may be decorated with a cloth hanging, typically in the liturgical color of the day. The pulpit is normally located on the Gospel (left-hand) side of the chancel or nave. For acoustical reasons, pulpits built in older churches were located against a wall or pier. Wherever it is located, it is crucial that the preacher be able to see and be seen by the entire congregation.

Some modern churches combine pulpit and lectern into a single furnishing called an ambo, from which both reading and preaching takes place. Some smaller churches do quite well without a pulpit, the preacher using the lectern or standing in the aisle.

Dearmer recommends the installation of a small clock within the pulpit: "The congregation will often have cause to be grateful if there is a clock within sight of the preacher."

In the American Episcopal Church Book of Common Prayer form for the Consecration of a Church, the new pulpit is blessed by the bishop with a prayer for those who preach and those who hear the Word of God from it. The pulpit thus stands as a symbol of God's presence in his Word, much as the altar symbolizes God's presence in the Holy Eucharist.

LECTERN _____

Toward the front of most churches built upon catholic designs there is some sort of stand on which an open copy of the Bible rests. This stand is called a lectern, from the Latin "legere," a verb meaning "to read."

A lectern is a stand, commonly made of wood or metal, on which the Bible and/or other liturgical books are placed in church. The top comprises a sort of bookstand, often with a lip to keep the books, which are inclined toward the reader, from slipping off. The normal height is about four feet, so as not to come between the head of the lector and the congregation. Higher lecterns, found in some churches, are designed primarily for cantors and not properly used for reading to the people.

Ornate lecterns are sometimes made in the form of an eagle or a pelican with its wings outspread so as to hold up the open Bible. The eagle is a symbol for St. John the Evangelist and is also a general symbol for the inspiration of the Gospel and of all of Holy Scripture. It is in this latter sense that eagles are well used to uphold the Bible read in public worship.

The typical placement of a lectern is in the front of the nave opposite the pulpit. Seen from the congregation, the lectern is on the right-hand (Epistle) side of the chancel and the pulpit on the left-hand (Gospel) side. The lectern is normally on a higher level than the floor of the nave, level with the choir. Absolute rules do not exist. At Durham Cathedral, in medieval times, the lectern was located at the north end of the high altar.

Hangings of cloth, often matching the frontal on the altar and the celebrant's vestments, are sometimes placed on the lectern. If the lectern is rectangular, the hangings are most often a square or rectangle of cloth. If it is an eagle, a stole (similar to clergy stoles) is sometimes draped from its neck. The use of cloths on a lectern is ancient. One record at Salisbury (Sarum) Cathedral says that the lectern there, in the form of an eagle, was decorated with such a cloth in 1222.

The importance of the lectern is self-evident. The American Episcopal Book of Common Prayer provides a special service for the Dedication and Consecration of a Church which includes the blessing of the lectern by a bishop (pp. 570-1). Thereafter, the Holy Bible, standing open on a lectern, symbolizes the presence of Jesus Christ—the Word of God—in Holy Scripture as it is read and revered in the church.

CREDENCE TABLE

Standing to one side of the altar in many churches is a table small enough not to detract from the centrality of the altar while large enough to hold many of the sacred vessels used in preparing to celebrate the Holy Eucharist. This is called a credence table.

The name derives from the Latin verb "credere" which means to trust or believe in. There is some evidence that the name for this liturgical table was first used to describe a side table (called a "credentia") used to taste the food to be served to a nobleman in order to ascertain that it was not poisoned. The person who tasted the food was called the "credentiarius." If the taster survived, a lord could trust or believe in the food, hence "credence."

The use of a side table, as distinct from a niche in the wall, dates generally from the 13th century. Ancient churches in England can be found with small shelves built into the sanctuary wall which apparently served as credences. Some authorities hold that English churches did well with neither.

There is good evidence of the use of a credence table in Sarum (Salisbury) Cathedral before the English Reformation. There exists some documentary evidence of the "reintroduction" of the use of the credence table during the reign of Elizabeth I. Such luminaries as Bishops Lancelot Andrewes and William Laud commended their use in the 17th century. A credence table is normally constructed of wood and stands on the sanctuary floor on the Epistle side. It is customarily covered with a white linen cloth, the ends of which hang over the table's sides. This covering is traditionally removed after the stripping of the altar on Maundy Thursday and restored at the Great Vigil of Easter.

For the last 500 years, the following have been placed on the credence table before the Holy Eucharist begins: the cruets of wine and water, the hosts in a bread box, the lavabo bowl and towel. In Eucharists where there is no procession of the oblations (bread and wine), this remains the practice. The rubrics in the American Book of Common Prayer require that the gifts of bread and wine be brought up to the altar by representatives of the congregation as part of the offertory. Although this appears to reduce the necessity of a credence table, it remains the traditional practice, even when there is an oblations procession, to place the cruet of water, the lavabo bowl and towel on the credence table before the chalice is prepared and to leave both cruets and the bread box there after the preparation.

ALTAR RAIL

Altar rails are a creature of the Protestant Reformation. It is not that the protestants required them. It is rather that they were constructed as a reaction when the protestants tore down the screens which separated the sanctuary from the chancel. During the Elizabethan Settlement, chancel screens were replaced by altar rails in English churches.

The Bishop of Norwich ordered, in 1636, that "a rayle be made before the Communion Table reaching cross from the North wall to the South wall, neere one yarde in height, so thick with pillars that dogges may not gett in." Many spiritualized explanations may be offered to explain the presence of altar rails, but the fact remains that their earliest functions were to keep wandering dogs from fouling the altar.

The earliest forms of English altar rails were typically known as "Laudian" after Archbishop William Laud, who promoted their use. These rails ran straight across the chancel to separate it from the sanctuary. Later, in some churches rails enclosed the altar area on three sides.

Seventeenth century English altar rails are often supported on turned pillars. The pillars came to be decorated with symbols of the Holy Eucharist, e.g. grape vines and stalks of wheat.

There is normally an opening at the center-front of an altar rail which may be closed with a gate made of the same material as the rail, or by a metal chain or velvet cord. If the latter are used, a metal device bearing some symbol is often suspended from the center of the closure.

Roman Catholic churches often include altar rails, more often called "communion rails" in light of their function, but in neither Anglican nor Roman Catholic use is an altar rail required. Its function might well be met in some churches by kneelers set atop a step which separates the sanctuary from the chancel or nave.

Those who have difficulty kneeling are sometimes assisted up and down by a hand on the altar rail. A baby brought to the sanctuary to receive a priestly blessing during the communion of the people may also be conveniently propped on the altar rail. In order that either of these auxiliary functions may be adequately performed, the altar rail must be well designed, of sturdy construction, in good repair, and of sufficient strength to bear whatever weight is placed upon it.

BAPTISMAL FONT _____

The sacrament of Holy Baptism is the door through which entry to the Body of Christ is gained. Thus, baptismal fonts are located near the door to the church as a visual symbol of this entrance for all baptized Christians. The term "font" derives from a Latin word "fons" meaning spring of water, a possible reference to the earlier custom of baptizing in running water.

The earliest baptismal fonts were probably tubs, vats or tanks which were sometimes tiled and decorated with baptismal symbols. In the cold climate of Northern Europe, where immersion was often less than practical, smaller fonts appropriate to sprinkling or pouring evolved. These were constructed of wood, stone or lead. Those of wood were lined with a stone or metal bowl to hold baptismal water. There is an earlier tradition that fonts should be of stone because Moses drew water from the rock in the wilderness. Some authority in English canon law supports this, but was never widely followed.

The decoration of baptismal fonts has derived from the images of water and baptism in the Holy Scriptures: John the Baptist, the baptism of our Lord, the four rivers of Paradise, and the hart (see Psalm 41). Celtic designs, particularly of knotted cording, appear on English fonts into the 11th century. The association of baptism with new life led English stone and wood sculptors to carve leaf patterns into them. Although pre-Reformation English stone fonts were often brightly colored, protestant reaction resulted in many of them being scraped and whitewashed, so that these colors and designs are lost forever.

In medieval times, baptismal water was not changed after each baptism, and a cover and a lock had to be provided to prevent the superstitious use of the water. Such latches are still in evidence on fonts dating from the 13th century.

In Great Britain, baptismal fonts dating from the 11th century are still in use. Norman fonts were often replaced during the 15th century, but many of these have been restored and replaced. During the Commonwealth, numerous fonts were removed from English churches and destroyed. Others, used as watering troughs for barnyard animals, have been reclaimed and reconsecrated.

In the American Episcopal prayer book, the form for the Consecration of a Church provides that the bishop bless the new font by laying his hand upon it and praying for all those who will be baptized there. The prayer asks "Grant through your Spirit that those baptized here may enjoy the liberty and splendor of the children of God."

PEWS

Pews can be constructed to be comfortable, numerous examples to the contrary notwithstanding. Before complaining too much about the habitability of modern pews, one should remember that they are a relatively recent innovation and an alternative to standing.

The two postures common to lay people in the early church were standing and kneeling. This is still the practice in many Eastern Orthodox Churches.

The early Christian churches provided no seating for members of the congregation, except an occasional stone bench against the wall for the infirm.

Wooden benches first appeared in English churches in the 13th century, but there is some evidence that their use was restricted to women and the elderly. The use of simple pews was common by the 15th century. The notion that pews had to be added because of the length of protestant sermons is untrue.

The term "pew" was first used to describe an elevated seat in a church, reserved for a dignitary. In the 17th century, medieval pews were discarded in favor of low boxes with built-in cushioned seats, some even covered with a canopy or tester. These boxes were reserved for the nobility and well-to-do. Commoners sat on benches.

As with all other church furnishings, the use of pews resulted in their elaboration and decoration. In England, it was common to carve the wooden bench-ends which faced the main aisle. A high art was achieved in this work, which can be seen in extant pew woodwork from 15th century East Anglia. English woodcarvers typically used, as their subjects, the passion of our Lord, events in the lives of saints, and some odd animals not part of modern zoology. The size of pews from the Tudor period suggests that people were smaller in those days than they are today.

Other than in size, the modern pew has changed too little from its antecedents. Some are designed with cushioned seats; the more common uncushioned variety may be improved by the addition of seat cushions. Pews should be so placed in relation to each other as to afford ample room for walking in and out, and for kneeling. Pews in the liturgical churches afford kneelers which fold down from the pew in front of the worshiper.

The use of pews brings with it immobility and regimentation to a congregation. This is an unavoidable evil which must be overcome liturgically with efforts to involve the congregation in the worship.

KNEELER _____

In the earliest English churches, parishioners kneeled on the stone or dirt floor. This arrangement was hard on the knees, hard on clothing and hard to endure, perhaps adding to the penitential symbolism of kneeling.

An intermediate improvement was the kneeling cushion, a sort of pillow resting freely on the floor. Kneeling cushions are still in use for the comfort of some liturgical ministers. They are also sometimes used at an altar rail.

In those churches with boxed pews, the families which occupied them were expected to provide their own cushions for kneeling, with the result that many fancy private kneelers were created and became a symbol of the status of the persons occupying a private pew.

The modern kneeler is most often a padded rail, so hinged and fitted into the pew ahead of the worshiper as to be folded down for kneeling on and folded up for entering and leaving the pew. Other typical modern kneelers are free standing (not affixed to the pew in front) and are built more like little padded benches.

Older kneelers were of wood, serving no greater

function than to raise the congregant's knees off the cold stone floor. Padded kneelers have since become the norm, often upholstered in a durable fabric in a color which harmonizes with the interior of the nave. With the resurgence of interest in needlepoint in the 20th century, some kneelers are now covered by beautiful and significant designs, often matching or complementing those on the kneeling cushions at the altar rail.

Especially elegant kneelers sometimes feature carved designs in the wooden end facing the central aisle of the church. Animal motifs are common, carrying out a theme of giving them "feet." As pews became common in England in the 15th century, providing an opportunity for the wood-carver's art, kneelers kept pace and some excellent examples of 15th and 16th century carving on the ends of kneelers survived the destruction wrought by the Puritans.

Modern kneelers tend to be more functional than decorative. A good kneeler promotes what it is for: assisting the worshiper in assuming a posture which is conducive to prayer.

It is a matter of etiquette that kneelers should never be left folded down when one leaves the pew, in order that the next person to enter may have easier access to a seat. It is also important to raise and lower kneelers quietly, so as not to disturb the prayers and meditations of one's neighbors.

CATHEDRA

In most cathedrals and in many parish churches, there is often an impressive-looking empty chair. This is the bishop's throne.

An Episcopal throne has been used in Christian

churches since ancient times. In the West, it was called "cathedra"; in the East, "sedes episcopi." The earliest of these were no more than chairs. The Peace of Constantine and the resultant equation between bishops of the church and princes of the state inspired the making of true thrones for bishops.

The earliest cathedra were of wood or stone but, from the 5th century, they became more elaborate and ornate: carved, bejeweled, inserted with ivory and precious metals.

The classic cathedra are of three parts—the platform on which the throne sits, the throne itself, and the canopy suspended above it. The platform raises the bishop's chair higher than the floor. The chair is of imposing proportions, with arms and a back higher than the top of the bishop's miter when he is seated. The canopy is sometimes decorated with the coat-of-arms of the bishop or the diocese.

Although there is considerable variation, the cathedra is most often located within the sanctuary near the main altar.

Such chairs have been much venerated. The Chair of Augustine is preserved at Canterbury Cathedral. Likewise, at Jarrow-on-Tyne, a seat known as the Chair of Bede is kept. Contemporary records of the desecration of English churches during the protestant reign include descriptions of "pluckynge downe" the thrones of bishops. After the Reformation, it was customary to put a chair of domestic design within the altar rail to provide episcopal seating.

Enthronement of a new bishop occurs when he takes his rightful place, seated in his new cathedral. The term cathedra properly refers only to the bishop's seat in a cathedral. The practice of setting aside a special chair for the bishop in a parish or mission church arose only in the 19th century and has been criticized on the theory that, during visitation, the bishop should sit in the presider's (celebrant's) chair. But there is a sense in which the bishop's chair in every parish and mission serves an important teaching function. The bishop is the rector of every mission and the chief pastor of every parish. His chair can be a reminder of this truth.

Ministers

Deacon

Acolyte

Thurifer

Lay Reader

Lector

Lay Eucharistic Ministers

Greeters

Altar Guild

Verger

DEACON

The ministry of Christ and of his Church is carried out by all baptized persons. The Church, from its beginning, has called upon persons to conduct specialized ministries within the larger Body of Christ. These include those in three holy orders: bishops, priests and deacons.

Sacred tradition holds that the order of deacons derives from the commissioning of the seven described in Acts 6:1-6, but the word "deacon" appears nowhere in this account. St. Stephen, the first martyr, and his six companions were called by the apostles to serve the poor, to visit the sick, to distribute alms and the like.

Elsewhere in the New Testament, true deacons appear (see Phil. 1:1; 1 Tim. 3:8-13). Later, in the writings of the Church Fathers, deacons appear as a separate, third order of ordained ministry, along with bishops and priests.

The Greek word for deacon means literally "servant" and early deacons exercised both liturgical and pastoral servant ministries. In the liturgy, they read the Gospel, called the people to prayer, assisted in Holy Baptism and in the distribution of Holy Eucharist. In the community, the deacons received and distributed the gifts of the people, and visited the sick and the poor.

"The ministry of a deacon is," according to the catechism in the American Book of Common Prayer, "to represent Christ and his Church, particularly as a servant to those in need; and to assist bishops and priests in the proclamation of the Gospel and the administration of the sacraments" (BCP p. 856). In the Western Church, ordination to the diaconate was until recent times mainly a step toward ordination to the priesthood. The traditional vestments of deacons—a garment called a dalmatic and a stole worn across the left shoulder—were soon exchanged for chasuble and a stole crossed priest-wise.

The protestant churches use the term deacon differently than it is used in the orthodox and catholic churches. It may often be used to describe a non-ordained person who functions as a pastoral assistant.

ACOLYTE

The ministry of acolytes is one of assisting those who perform the liturgies of the Church. Acolytes assist the bishops, priests, deacons and other lay ministers conducting a liturgy by acting like good waiters in a restaurant, nurses in a surgery or attendants in a cloakroom. They assist the congregation by acting as examples of when to do what in the service. Their ministry is always marked by servanthood and is thus an authentic ministry of Christ.

There is historical evidence of this office in the 3rd century in both Rome and Carthage. For many centuries, the office was one of the four minor orders (along with porter, lector, and exorcist) in the Roman Catholic Church. In the Eastern Church, they were subsumed by the subdiaconate.

Liturgical purists suggest that the designation "acolyte" be restricted to the function of lighting, carrying and extinguishing candles, but the term is derived from a Latin word which means "follower" and is not sensibly so limited. The alternate term "server" is often used to describe persons who help with candles, carry a cross (crucifer) or an incenser (thurifer), or assist in other ways. The Roman term "altar boy" is no longer appropriate to Roman or Anglican Churches, with the admission of females to these ministries.

In typically Anglican fashion, the American Book of Common Prayer never mentions the word "acolyte" or "server." The rubrics for the Holy Eucharist do urge that the principal celebrant "be assisted by other priests, and by deacons and lay persons" (BCP pp. 322, 354). Acolytes are among those lay persons.

Individual acolytes and guilds within parishes often belong to the Order of Saint Vincent, a worldwide organization of people in lay liturgical ministries which promotes a sacramentally-based rule of life, intercessory prayer and the study of liturgics.

The English liturgist Percy Dearmer counseled that acolytes should "avoid all fuss and needless running about." For a fuller treatment of their roles, see *You Are an Acolyte* (Forward Movement Publications).

THURIFER

A thurifer is a person who carries a thurible. A thurible is a device (sometimes called a censer), usually suspended on chains, in which incense is burnt. These terms come from the Latin words "thuris" meaning frankincense (derived from the Greek word "thyos" meaning incense) and "thuribulum" meaning incense burner.

The thurifer is often an acolyte or altar server, but the role may be performed by anyone appointed.

Sometimes the thurifer also carries a container for additional incense called a "boat"; other times, this container is carried by someone historically known as a "boat boy" (regardless of sex). In those congregations where acolytes are younger people, the boat boy is often a thurifer-in-training.

The thurible is normally held in the right hand by

the chains. It is swung gently during processions to keep the charcoal lit and to cause the incense to burn. The amount of charcoal placed into the thurible at the beginning of the liturgy is rarely sufficient to last until the Offertory. Thus the thurifer must add charcoal at such times and in such amounts as to have the fire ready for the addition and use of incense at the appropriate moments. This task is made easier by the invention of self-lighting charcoal which is impregnated with paraffin or some other readily-combustible matter. These compressed bits light themselves quickly and easily from the still-burning bits in the thurible.

Processions in which incense is used are led by the thurifer, who precedes even the crucifer and attending acolytes. The censer is most often swung fore and aft during procession. Sometimes an accomplished thurifer will swing the thurible in a complete circle which increases both the dispersion of the smoke and the dramatic impact of its use.

While some thurifers become quite accomplished at their tasks, the use of incense is not a performance to showcase the operator's talents but a solemn and reverent offering to God.

It is also a thurifer's duty to dispose of the still-burning coals at the conclusion of the liturgy in such a fashion that the church does not burn down before the next service.

LAY READER _____

It is sometimes surprising to visitors to an Episcopal Church to discover that one or more of the leaders of the worship service, vested in about the same manner as clergy, are lay persons. These ministers are often licensed lay readers. They serve in a ministry as ancient as the Church.

One part of the heritage in which lay readers minister is the office of reader, found in both the 1st century synagogue and the early Christian Church. Another part of the heritage of American lay readers derives from the colonial and frontier experience when there were insufficient clergy to lead the worship of Episcopal congregations. American lay readers conducted Morning and Evening Prayer as best they could.

The first lay readers licensed in the Church of England were admitted in 1866. They led Morning and Evening Prayer in churches without clergy or where the clergy required assistance. A few were actually salaried!

The first American prayer book of 1789 allowed lay readers to read the Epistle at Holy Communion. Under the 1928 American prayer book, they were permitted little else. The role of lay readers was vastly expanded by the 1979 American Book of Common Prayer.

There have been times when licensed lay readers have been made responsible for the liturgical (and sometimes pastoral) leadership of a congregation when clergy were not available. Lay readers have also performed many other functions usually associated with clergy: teaching catechism, preaching, and visiting the sick. This has led to the erroneous notion that they are junior-grade clergy.

For many years, the license for lay readers was available only to men. In 1969, the first women lay readers were licensed in the Church of England. The American canon was amended in 1973 to allow "persons" to be licensed.

The present canon governing lay readers also

governs the many ministries of lay pastoral leaders, lay preachers, lay eucharistic ministers, lay catechists, and lectors. Each of these ministries, except that of lectors, requires a license from the bishop. Each is open to confirmed adult men and women who regularly attend and contribute to the support of their church. The canon requires that lay readers be trained, examined and licensed to "regularly lead public worship."

LECTOR

The Old Testament book of Nehemiah tells the story of an assembly of the people in which the prophet brings out the book of the Law of Moses and reads it to them. He is assisted by others who also read the law aloud. (Nehemiah 8:3) This story prefigures the role of lectors (readers) in the Church.

Jesus fulfilled this office himself, setting a holy example for all lectors to follow (Luke 4:16-17). The early Christians adopted the synagogue practice of reading the scriptures aloud in their meetings (1 Tim. 4:13).

The antiquity of readers in the Church is attested to by the early fathers. St. Justin Martyr (ca. 150) mentions them, as do Tertullian (160-230), St. Cyprian (d. 258) and the Apostolic Constitutions (late 4th century), suggesting that the function, if not the office, of lector has been in the Church at least from the 2nd century.

In the Middle Ages, the order of lectors was "ordained" along with three other so-called minor orders: acolyte, exorcist and porter.

The modern office of lector is sometimes subsumed by that of lay readers licensed by the bishop. Lay readers are licensed to do a great deal more than read lessons (e.g. conduct entire services). The role of lector may be performed in the Episcopal Church by anyone asked by the celebrant or officiant to read a lesson or lead a psalm or the Prayers of the People. While this has been true for many years, the canons of the church were amended in 1988 to formalize this understanding of the role of the lector.

Genuine ministries arise from the gifts which are possessed by members of the Church. As the Spirit confers different gifts on different people, so the Church is supplied with all the ministers necessary to her tasks (1 Cor. 12:4-11). To be gifted with a good voice (which can be trained to sound even better) and a good sense of reading aloud (which can be trained to interpret even better) is to be equipped for the ministry of the lector.

It is a great privilege to be asked to read the lessons or lead the psalm in public worship. Anglicans believe that God the Holy Spirit speaks to individuals through Holy Scripture and that one of the ways in which he uses this medium is through the public reading of lessons and psalms.

LAY EUCHARISTIC MINISTERS _____

The ministry of lay persons in the celebration and administration of the Holy Eucharist has expanded in recent years. Under the 1928 American Book of Common Prayer, a lay person was allowed to read the epistle and nothing else. The opportunities for lay liturgical ministry in the 1979 prayer book were greatly increased. This opening included the administration of the chalice at Holy Eucharist by licensed lay persons "in the absence of sufficient deacons or priests" (rubric at BCP p. 408). No provision was made for the administration of the host by lay persons under any circumstances. People licensed under these rubrics were properly called "chalice bearers."

Nothing in the 1979 prayer book permitted lay persons to carry the elements to persons unable to be present at the celebration of the Holy Eucharist. The rubrics in the service of Communion Under Special Circumstances (BCP pp. 396-99) indicate that communion will be brought to the sick only by a bishop, priest or deacon.

The former canon which permitted the special licensing of those already licensed as lay readers to administer the chalice has been replaced by a comprehensive canon dealing with the licensing of lay persons to perform a variety of ministries. Under this canon, clergy in charge of a congregation may request that a lay person be licensed by the bishop as a lay eucharistic minister. Title III, canon 3, section 2 creates two different types of Lay Eucharistic Ministers. One is similar to the former chalice bearers, except that lay persons may now administer "the elements at any Celebration of the Holy Eucharist in the absence of a sufficient number of Priests or Deacons assisting the celebrant." The second permits licensed lay persons to carry "the Sacrament consecrated at a Celebration to . . . [people] unable to be present." This canon does not authorize lay eucharistic ministers to administer from the reserved sacrament but only to extend the celebration on a Sunday or principal holy day by taking the elements directly to those absent.

Diocesan bishops establish the qualifications, guidelines and requirements for selection and training of these persons, who may be licensed to perform either or both of the functions permitted by the canon. A lay eucharistic minister should normally be under the direction of a deacon of the congregation, if there is one.

GREETERS _____

It is common to be met at the door of a church on a Sunday morning by someone (or a family) who welcomes the newcomer, hands out the bulletins, invites visitors to sign a guest register, and shows people the way to the nursery, the Sunday school and the nave. Some of these functions were formerly performed by a corps of ushers—usually all men—who concentrated on getting people into the pews. The ministry of welcoming is performed by greeters. While the "office" of greeter is relatively new to the church, its antecedents extend to the customs of hospitality in ancient Israel.

From the point-of-view of the informality of American culture, the hospitality of the ancient Near East seems strange, elaborate and sometimes confusing. All the cultures in biblical times had a strict code of hospitality, the observance of which was demanded.

The stranger held a special place in the Israelite community. He was under the protection of God, and faithful Jews were required to treat him well (Lev. 19:33-34; Deut. 10:18-19). Because visitors in ancient Semitic communities had no legal or social standing, the patronage of a host was required.

Jesus was well familiar with his people's customs regarding hospitality. His story about the shepherd who separates the sheep from the goats (in Matthew 27:31-46) can only be fully understood if one understands the duties of a host to a stranger. Hospitality was frequently commended to early Christians (see e.g. Romans 12:13 and 1 Peter 4:9). The recipient of Near Eastern hospitality then praised his host to his friends on account of his good treatment.

One of the four minor orders of ordained ministry in the early Church was called "porter" or "ostiari."

Porters functioned like a doorkeeper. The order was probably established in the 3rd century. The primary function of porters appears to have been excluding the unbaptized from the Holy Eucharist.

While the modern ministry of greeter draws little from the tradition of porters, it can be seen in light of Jewish customs of hospitality. The stranger holds a special place in the Christian community. The community provides a host to extend its hospitality to the newcomer and visitor. The recipient of warm hospitality is likely to tell his or her friends.

Greeters would do well to take the story of the three men who visited Sarah and Abraham (Genesis 18:1-15) as an excellent example: one never knows when one might be entertaining angels.

ALTAR GUILD

In traditional Japanese theatre, persons dressed all in black come onto the stage, move scenery and props, and withdraw—without being "seen" by the audience. While these stage hands are visible in the physical sense, they are invisible by convention. The role of such people is similar to that of the ministry of members of an altar guild.

The early Christians probably celebrated their Holy Eucharists in the homes of members. After the establishment of the Christian Church by Constantine, the Eucharist was moved into large buildings where the preparations were more elaborate.

Throughout most of Christian history, the care and preparation of things to be used in worship was the duty of a sacristan who was always male and sometimes in minor orders. The modern altar guild did not evolve until the late 19th century.

The duties of the altar guild vary from place to place, based on what has been done there in the past. Some are in charge of the vestments to be used by the clergy (or by all the ministers who vest for worship). Others are responsible for cleaning the church. Some specialize in arranging flowers for the sanctuary while others see to it that this is professionally done. Setting up the vessels with which to celebrate the Holy Eucharist is done by members of an altar guild in many churches; a deacon performs this task in a few. Needlework done by altar guilds has produced everything from whole sets of vestments and hangings to the lavabo and baptismal towels.

In those parishes with a worship committee, a representative of the altar guild should always be a member. This representative will link liturgical planning with the nuts-and-bolts of preparing the worship space and equipment.

Every Episcopal diocese in the United States has a diocesan altar guild which provides both educational and service ministries. These are represented in a national altar guild which assists the Presiding Bishop in similar ministries.

The ministry of the altar guild is recognized as an important ministry of the church by a service of commissioning in the Book of Occasional Services.

Another recognition of the particular ministry of altar guilds occurs in those parishes where a corporate communion of the members of the guild occurs every year on Maundy Thursday, which celebrates the institution of the Lord's Supper.

VERGER

Worshipers accustomed to seeing all processions led by the crucifer bearing a processional cross are sometimes surprised when a verger, carrying a rod or mace, leads the procession in a cathedral or larger parish church.

The term verger derives from the mace carried before a ruler or dignitary, from the Latin "virga" meaning a twig, rod or wand. The mace originated as a club, sometimes with spikes on one end, used to penetrate medieval armor. The mace grew to have symbolic meaning as a sign of official authority; the design of the mace or rod changed accordingly.

The distinction between civil and sacred authority was much less clear in the Middle Ages than it is today. Thus the "verge" came to be carried before ecclesiastical dignitaries. In the Sarum rite, as it existed before the English Reformation, processions were led by a verger, vested and carrying his mace or verge.

While a verge often looks a great deal like a staff, it ought not be confused with a warden's staff, which is more like a walking stick and is used by churchwardens in procession.

The role of the verger has grown to mean not only the person who carries the verge before a bishop or dean in procession, but also a church caretaker and/or an usher. In some English churches there can be found a verger's cupboard, which is more like a closet in which are kept the verger's gown and mace, as well as alms bags or plates for the offering. The role of the verger has sometimes been filled by others: a sexton or a sacristan, a church warden, or even (once, at Lincoln Cathedral) by the cathedral carpenter and glazier!

It is traditional in congregations served by a verger that he conduct the preacher to the pulpit. In grandest fashion, a verger carries his mace to the preacher's stall in the chancel, leads the preacher to the steps to the pulpit and, if there is a door to the steps, opens and closes it for him.

There is a great variety of verger's gowns. They are commonly black but sometimes blue or even crimson. They are traditionally trimmed in black velvet, in two panels down the front, sometimes at the collar, and occasionally (like large chevrons) on the sleeves.

Far from being in danger of extinction, the office of verger is growing in the United States where a national guild of vergers was recently formed, after the fashion of a more ancient guild in Great Britain.

Vestments

Alb

Amice

Chasuble

Cope

Girdle/Cincture

Cassock

Surplice/Cotta

Stole

Tippet

Hood

Rings

ALB

The alb (or in older English "albe") is a full-length garment with narrow sleeves extending from the neck to the ankles. Before the invention of synthetic fabrics, albs were made of white linen, although silk albs were in use in well-to-do parishes and cathedral churches. At one time, the alb was worn over a cassock and was of sufficient length to cover that vestment entirely.

The alb derives from the Greco-Roman undertunic which was worn as street clothing in the Roman Empire. Its use as a eucharistic vestment is reminiscent of the clean white tunic in which the early Christians were dressed when they emerged naked from the waters of Holy Baptism. The alb's white color is symbolic of purity.

This baptismal symbol is maintained by the traditional vesting prayer, said while putting on the alb: "Cleanse me, O Lord, and purify my heart, that washed in the Blood of the Lamb, I may attain everlasting joy."

Traditional albs are collarless and worn with the amice. These have been largely replaced with albs with built-in collars or hoods once called amice-albs but now so common that the reference to the sewn-in amice is omitted.

The alb may be decorated with lace at the hem and cuffs, or it may be decorated with strips of embroidered fabric (such as damask) sewn along the hem which are called "apparels." An appareled amice is often worn to match the appareled alb. Appareled albs date from the 11th century.

The alb may be worn girdled or ungirdled. The common girdle or cincture is a cord or band of fabric worn like a belt around the waist of the alb. Girdling makes the most sense when worn with a cassock-alb, an alb cut like a double-breasted (Anglican) cassock.

The use of the alb in Anglican worship is attested by records of the inventories of English cathedrals prior to the Reformation. Both Winchester and Canterbury Cathedrals had large stocks of white albs, mostly of silk. The 1549 English Book of Common Prayer provided that the celebrant at Holy Eucharist shall wear "a white albe plain."

The ordinal of 1550 required that those to be ordained deacon or priest be vested in alb. The American Prayer Book directs that the candidate for ordination as a bishop be vested in alb or rochet and a candidate for ordination as deacon or priest be vested in alb or surplice. The alb is not, however, strictly a clerical vestment. It may properly be worn by all persons acting as ministers in a celebration of the Holy Eucharist—acolytes, lay eucharistic ministers, choristers, servers, and the like.

AMICE

Liturgical vestments, while many derive from early Roman secular dress, are subject to all manner of fashions. The use of the amice in America is currently out of fashion.

An amice (pronounced AM-iss) is a large square or rectangular piece of linen folded about the neck and shoulders to form a collar for the alb, with which it is worn.

While several modern dictionaries describe it as worn by a priest, it may be worn by any liturgical minister who is also wearing an alb. There is some medieval evidence that the amice was presented by the bishop to a subdeacon at his ordination as one of the vestments of his office.

The name amice may derive from the Latin

"amictus" meaning cloak or from the Latin "amicio" meaning to wrap around. It is sometimes confused with the almuce, a fur-lined hood worn by clerics and religious since the 12th century, and which is still in evidence in some monastic orders and among canons in France.

The amice is not used in the Eastern Church. In the West, its use dates reliably from the 8th century. Since about the 10th century, it has been placed over the head like a hood and then folded into a collar. This makes sense of the traditional vesting prayer said while putting on the amice: "Place, O Lord, the helmet of salvation upon my head, to repel the assaults of the devil." This prayer is an obvious reference to the metaphor in Ephesians 6:17 in which the armor of God, including the "helmet of salvation," is put on to repel the devil. This allusion is also paralleled in 1 Thessalonians 5:8, and both references are probably derived from a similar analogy in Isaiah 59:17. In some religious orders, the amice is unfolded and pulled up over the head when the wearer approaches the altar.

The modern amice is made with strings attached to secure it in place. These strings are very long and are crossed over the chest and tied around the waist.

Most amices are plain but may occasionally be appareled, which is to say that a piece of damask silk, colored to match the outer vestments, is sewn onto the outside of the collar.

One practical value of the amice is that it protects the more expensive vestments from hair oils, which may be more easily washed from linen than dry-cleaned from stoles and chasubles.

The modern use of a separate amice is dwindling, as most albs have a built-in collar or hood, or are so constructed as to appear as if an amice is being worn.

CHASUBLE

The chasuble is the sleeveless outermost vestment worn by the celebrant over the alb at Holy Eucharist. It may be worn by priest or bishop, but not by a deacon, because deacons may administer but do not celebrate the Holy Eucharist.

The term "chasuble" is related to an Old French word "casula" meaning a hooded garment, and to an older Latin word "casula" which was a diminutive of "casa" meaning cottage, little house or tent.

The garment itself is related to the "paenula" or "planets" of the 1st century Greco-Roman world where it was a poncho-like cloak with a hole in the center for the head.

The first liturgical use of this "vestment" was probably by a priest or bishop who wore it in the 1st century as street-clothing. It soon became the principal eucharistic vestment of the church.

The chasuble was in common use in England in 1549 at the time of the first Book of Common Prayer. The more protestant book of 1552 prohibited its use on the theory that it was "popish" and "Romish." The Ornaments Rubric in the 1559 prayer book (re-enacted in 1661) re-established the chasuble, but it fell into disuse in the Church of England until its restoration in the 19th century.

In typical American Episcopal fashion, the use of the chasuble is neither prescribed nor proscribed by the canons nor by the Book of Common Prayer. According to the ordination rubrics a newly-ordained priest is "vested according to the order of priests" (BCP p. 534). It is common to place the chasuble on the ordinand.

The Holy Eucharist may properly be celebrated with or without the chasuble, as is appropriate to time, place, occasion and local custom. Older practice suggested that it be worn only during the liturgy of the table (never in procession and never in the pulpit), thus the typical practice of vesting the celebrant in the chasuble during the offertory.

Chasubles may be constructed of silk damask, tapestry, velvet, brocade, linen or cloth of gold. They may be made primarily in the liturgical colors (frequently to match other hangings in a set) or in more all-purpose colors. A white chasuble may be decorated with orphreys or borders in another liturgical color. An orphrey is a strip or band of colored cloth, often embroidered, which may form a cross or letter "Y" on the front or back of a chasuble. As celebrants now tend to face the congregation, decoration on modern chasubles seems to be migrating from their backs to their fronts.

COPE

A cope looks much like a chasuble (and, in fact, derives from the same original Roman garment) but, unlike a chasuble, is open in the front. The two sides of the cope are often held together by a device called a morse. A morse is a clasp, made of cloth or metal, which is often highly decorated.

Copes originally had functional hoods attached at the back of the neck; vestiges of these may appear on modern copes in the form of triangular folded hoods which ornament their backs.

Research in old carvings, paintings and mosaics depicting the clergy establish that the cope was worn as a liturgical vestment as early as the 6th century. Gregory of Tours (ca. 540-594) refers to this vestment as the "cappa."

In the Middle Ages, a black cappa, made of heavy wool, evolved and became known as the cappa nigra, which is still worn today, often over cassock and surplice when the minister is required to function out-of-doors during winter.

Rubrics in the 1549 English prayer book required the celebrant at the Holy Eucharist to vest in either cope or chasuble. This rubric was omitted from the 1552 revision. A canon was adopted in the Church of England in 1604 which required that the celebrant at Eucharist in a cathedral church or college chapel vest in cope. There is no evidence that this canon was ever universally observed. Since the mid-19th century, a renewed interest in historic vestments has led to the much-restored use of the cope in Anglican churches.

Traditional copes are made of silk or brocade; modern designs use many other fabrics to great advantage: tapestry, cloth of gold, velvet, and other sorts of cloth. Traditional copes are frequently richly decorated with orphreys, fringe, tassels and even icons sewn onto them. Modern copes are perhaps a bit more reserved.

There is no requirement that a cope be in the liturgical color of the season or occasion; thus copes in many hues, particularly of gold, are common.

The cope is often worn by a priest or bishop in procession and then exchanged for the chasuble at the altar. Although the cope is not in any sense an "episcopal" vestment, they are most often seen worn by bishops because most congregations can ill afford them.

The cope is particularly appropriate to major feasts, highly festal celebrations, at weddings and burials, at solemn Te Deum or Great Litany sung or said in procession, during the Liturgy of the Palms on Palm Sunday, and in Rogation processions.

GIRDLE/CINCTURE _____

Many Christian liturgical vestments mimic the street clothes of 1st century Roman citizens. At the time of Christ, a cord or sash was worn as a belt over the outer clothing to hold the robes together. From this belt the girdle and cincture developed.

The terms "girdle" and "cincture" are used interchangeably, but traditional manuals distinguish them. The girdle is a long cord or rope while the cincture is a wide sash. Generally an alb is closed with a girdle, an Anglican-style double-breasted cassock is closed with a cincture, and a Roman cassock is closed with either one.

The girdle is always worn with the alb in the Western Church. The Eastern Church requires that bishops and priests girdle their albs; deacons wear theirs unbelted.

The traditional girdle is ten to twelve feet long, is made of linen, flax or silk, and is circular in cross-section. It is worn doubled so that a noose is formed at one end through which the free ends pass and extend almost to the floor.

Typical modern girdles are white to match the albs with which they are worn. There is some English authority, as old as the 13th century, for wearing girdles in the liturgical color of the day. An inventory conducted at Aberdeen Cathedral in 1559 showed that it possessed five blue-and-white girdles and one of green silk.

The evidence of church brasses suggests that the cincture worn in medieval times was a buckled belt. Later cinctures were closed with laces in the back. A still later custom was to join the ends with three buttons at the side. Some modern cinctures are equipped with Velcro closures!

The modern cincture is generally made either of a fabric which matches the cassock or of lined silk. It is typically 3 $\frac{1}{2}$ yards long and 4 $\frac{1}{2}$ to 6 inches wide. The ends of the cincture hang to the hem of the cassock and are often finished in either tassels for dignitaries or fringe for ordinary priests.

Christ referred to the girdle as a symbol of preparation and readiness for service (Luke 12:35-38). St. Paul referred to it as a symbol of truth (Ephesians 6:14). The girdle of the monastic habit, knotted three times at the ends, symbolizes the three vows of poverty, chastity and obedience. The girdle became a Christian symbol of chastity, possibly derived from the ancient Jewish custom of women wearing ornate girdles symbolic of their virtue (Proverbs 31). Some traditional clergy still use an old vesting prayer when putting on the girdle which says, "Gird me, O Lord, with the girdle of purity, and quench in me the fire of concupiscence, that the grace of temperance and chastity may abide in me."

CASSOCK

The cassock is a long, somewhat snug, commonly black gown with sleeves worn either by itself or underneath the cotta or surplice. It is worn by clergy, lay readers, choristers, and acolytes. The use of the cassock is very ancient; it descends from the "vestis talaris" worn by the clergy in the 6th century. The English word "cassock" comes from the French "casaque" and the Italian "casacca" which means "housecoat."

There are two principal styles of cassocks: Roman and Anglican, or Sarum. The Roman cassock is single-breasted with buttons up the front, cuffed, without a cape and normally made of wool. The Anglican cassock is double-breasted, buttoned at the shoulder and held together with a band worn like a belt, called a cincture. Another type of cassock is the soutane, which has a short cape sewn into the collar, with buttons up the front, which is worn on occasions outside of the church. The use of the soutane is not common among Anglicans. In the Eastern Church, the "rason" corresponds to the Western cassock, although it looks a bit more like an academic gown.

An Anglican bishop's cassock traditionally is made of purple cloth with crimson linings, buttons and cuffs. In penitential seasons, bishops sometimes wear black cassocks with purple silk linings, buttons and cuffs. The bishop's cincture is the same color as the cassock. Until the last century, Anglican bishops wore this attire in the office as well as in the church.

The Anglican canons of 1604 required clergy to wear a cassock as part of their street clothes. Up until the beginning of the 19th century, English clerics wore cassocks abroad. There is an old story about a Spanish traveler who came to England in 1810 and was surprised to find that the English clergy were "all dressed like Benedictine monks"!

Roman Catholics follow a strict color-scheme for cassocks—black for priests, violet for bishops, red for cardinals and white for the Pope. Anglicans have not followed this practice. One English church manual from the 1930s favored dark grey, medium grey and blue for wear in England and white or buff cotton for wear in the warmer colonies. The most common colors for cassocks in the United States are black, red (for acolytes) and violet (for bishops and canons).

The use of the cassock in the American Episcopal Church is entirely a matter of tradition. There are no canons or rubrics directing who may wear what sort of vestment when and where. The cassock remains the normative vestment for all ministers taking part in a service.

SURPLICE/COTTA

Of all the liturgical vestments, probably none is as beautiful as a fully-cut and flowing surplice. The surplice is a long white vestment worn over the cassock on all occasions when an alb is not required. The surplice is always white, a symbol of purity. The best are made from fine cotton; modern blends wrinkle less easily, but are not equal to linen in quality or appearance.

The term surplice comes from the Latin "superpelliceum" which means "over a fur garment." The origin of the surplice is said to be as a substitute for the tighter-fitting alb which was unsuitable to wear over the fur coats necessary to winters in Northern Europe.

The length of pre-Reformation surplices can be measured from brass rubbings dating to that period in England. Early surplices were as long as albs, extending to the ankles. The surplice grew shorter and shorter until, by the 18th century, it became a cotta.

The cotta is a white vestment, similar to the surplice, which is cut shorter (about to the waist), is less full, with less ample sleeves and a neck cut squarely into a yoke. By the 18th century, the cotta was extremely popular among Roman Catholics. In reaction, English surplices remained long (below the knees), which vestments are now sometimes called Anglican surplices.

The cotta and surplice are sometimes completed with lace sewn to the lowest part. There are traditions concerning how much lace and from where it may extend. For example, one commentator holds that a priest should have no more than three or four inches of lace while a canon (clergy attached to a cathedral) may have lace from the waist to the knees.

Since about the 12th century, it has been normative for clergy to wear the surplice for all liturgies other than Holy Eucharist. In the 1552 English prayer book, the surplice was the only required clergy vestment. There was considerable fuss during the last half of the 16th century over the surplice. Protestants favored its abolition as Romish garb; catholics favored a restoration of all traditional eucharistic vestments such as the alb and chasuble. The canons of the Church of England (1969) require that the surplice be worn by clergy for Morning and Evening Prayer and the Occasional Offices. There is no such requirement in the American Church.

The modern surplice is worn by clergy and lay persons without regard to their order. The modern use of the cotta seems restricted to acolytes on whom it looks less like child's clothing worn by an adult. The surplice is properly worn by clergy for all services other than Holy Eucharist and by lay readers, members of choir, acolytes, servers and organists, at all services.

STOLE

A stole is a long, narrow strip of cloth worn by clergy as an emblem of ordination. The name derives from the Latin "stola." In the Eastern Church, a priest's stole is called "epitrachelion" and the deacon's stole is called "orarion."

Stoles have been worn by deacons since the 4th century in the East and since the 6th century in the

West. Priests adopted stoles shortly thereafter. Their use in the Church of England waned after the English Reformation but was restored in the 19th century.

The deacon's stole is commonly worn like a sash over the left shoulder with the ends tied or fastened under the right arm. The priest's stole is worn around the neck. The ends may be crossed in front or allowed to hang straight down. Until recently, the former was the style for priests and the latter for bishops.

The Eastern practice was to wear stoles over outer eucharistic vestments while the Western practice has been to wear a stole over the alb but under the dalmatic or chasuble. Some modern vestment sets include both a plain stole to be worn under and a more ornate stole to be worn over the principal vestment.

Stoles were traditionally made of silk but modern stoles are made in the same great variety of fabrics as are chasubles. They may be long or short, wide or narrow, highly ornamented or plain, and are sometimes completed with fringe. It used to be said that eucharistic stoles were longer than preaching stoles, so that the end could be seen under chasuble; this is a lost distinction.

Stoles were sometimes equipped with a piece of lace or linen at the neck to keep the oils from the priest's hair from discoloring the fabric of the stole. English ecclesiologist Percy Dearmer opposed the use of such "antimacassars" because "our clergy are cleanly in their habits."

A small cross may be embroidered at the back of the stole which some priests kiss before putting it on, sometimes while saying a vesting prayer.

The color of the stole is usually determined by the liturgical color of the season. The particular sacrament being conferred sometimes guides color selection, e.g. red for ordinations, white for weddings, and purple or violet for the reconciliation of a penitent. Some priests carry a small, ribbon-like stole with them on visitations, along with a communion kit and oil for anointing, wearing this stole over a shirt, blouse or jacket. Such stoles are often white on one side and purple or violet on the other.

Vestments are only rarely mentioned in the American Book of Common Prayer. The Celebration of a New Ministry suggests that one of the symbols presented to a new rector or vicar be a stole (p. 561).

TIPPET

The tippet is a long black scarf worn by Episcopal clergy over the white surplice (which is worn over the cassock). While tippets look a little bit like the stoles which clergy wear with alb at Holy Eucharist, they are quite distinct vestments with their own history and proper usage.

This attire—cassock, surplice and tippet—is known as "choir habit" because it is the appropriate form of vestment for the choir offices of Morning and Evening Prayer. Some English wags dubbed this habit "magpie" because its black and white coloring resembles that of the bird.

The tippet is often worn with an academic hood, the color, shape, material and design of which indicate the academic degree held by the wearer and the institution which granted the degree.

One theory of the origin of the tippet is that it comprised the front part of the academic hood, hanging in front while the hood hung in back. Another theory of the tippet's origin is that, like so many vestments, it derived from a secular garment worn of practical necessity. The chill of unheated English churches in winter suggests that a black woolen scarf might well have been wrapped around the neck (during the offices when a stole is not worn) just to keep the wearer warm.

The canons of 1604 required English clergy to wear the tippet as part of their everyday attire. It was common to see a priest in the streets wearing an academic gown, tippet and a square cloth cap. At that time, distinction was made between silken tippets, worn only by clergy with academic degrees, and woolen tippets which were worn by non-degreed clergy.

In some parts of the church, black stoles have been worn at the Burial Office and on Good Friday. Some clergy confused these black stoles with the tippet and wore them with their cassock and surplice. This error never gained wide usage and black stoles are practically nonexistent today.

Military chaplains (and former military chaplains) sometimes wear their military ribbons on the tippet, in about the same place where they would be located on the breast of the military tunic.

Modern tippets are sometimes ornamented with emblems sewn on the ends of the scarf. The red-white-and-blue shield of the Episcopal Church often appears on one end. Sometimes the shield of the theological school attended by the wearer is placed on the other.

HOOD

The modern academic hood is barely recognizable as a "hood" at all. It is more like a small cape, the narrow front band of which passes over the shoulders and across the upper chest, the rest of which hangs down the back to about the waist. A fold in this back portion is a vestigal hood. The fold allows the contrasting color of the lining to be seen.

The color, size, and materials of academic hoods are all of significance, but this significance has evolved over time and no fixed rules can be stated. The colors of the silk lining generally identify the granting institution. The colors of the velvet banding generally identify the field of study (e.g. arts and sciences, philosophy, law, medicine, theology). Doctoral hoods are generally larger than masters' hoods. During the 17th century, the master of arts hood from Oxford was readily identifiable in that it was fully lined with white fur!

Academic hoods were worn with cassock and surplice in what was called "choir habit" in pre-Reformation England. The canons at the time of the first English prayer book directed clergy to wear "such hood as pertaineth to their several degrees, which they may have taken in any university within this realm." It was also traditional for the preacher to vest in cassock, surplice, hood and tippet.

While there is neither rubric nor canon governing the wearing of the academic hood in the American Episcopal Church, by custom it is worn with cassock and surplice, never with the alb, at the choir offices of Morning and Evening Prayer, and when preaching at Holy Eucharist, unless vested in alb to celebrate or assist at the altar.

There is a sense in which an academic hood is not a liturgical vestment at all, but rather a scholastic vestment appropriate to be worn at commencement with an academic gown and mortar-board hat. What place does a symbol of the personal academic achievement of a clergy member have in liturgical vesture? While academic hoods have no ecclesiastical significance, they are traditional because there is a long tradition of educated clergy in Anglicanism. The canons of the American Church generally require a bachelor's degree of those seeking Holy Orders. Seminary graduates receive a master's degree, and many now earn a doctorate. The wearing of academic hoods is a symbol of the church's commitment to an educated clergy.

RINGS

From at least the 3rd and 4th centuries, both lay and ordained Christians have worn rings bearing Christian symbols. These likely evolved into the bishops' rings worn now by Anglican and Roman bishops.

Apart from this development, the early Church adapted the use of wedding rings (at least for brides) from the pagan Roman custom. In some religious orders, particularly those for women, a gold ring comparable to a wedding ring is conferred at the time the nun makes her life profession, symbolizing that she is now the bride of Christ.

A ring bearing the seal of the diocese is often presented to a newly-consecrated bishop as one of the emblems of office as part of the "vesting." Since late medieval times, the placing of the bishop's ring on his finger accompanied his investiture with other emblems of office such as a staff and a mitre. This practice of vesting was retained in the English ordinal of 1550 but mention of the ring was omitted. In the American Book of Common Prayer, following the consecration prayer, "the new bishop is . . . vested according to the order of bishops" (BCP P. 521). Although this rubric mentions no specific vestments, this is the time at which the episcopal ring is normally placed on the third finger of the new bishop's right hand.

Episcopal rings are normally made of gold and are set with an amethyst—the stone traditionally associated with the episcopate.

The ring of a bishop is used (1) practically, to seal documents such as ordination certificates, and (2) symbolically to signify betrothal to the Church, although not in a celibate sense.

Roman Catholic cardinals, abbots and abbesses may also wear a simpler version of the episcopal ring. Traditionally, a cardinal's ring is set with a sapphire.

A newly-elected Pope is "vested" with a fisherman's ring which is made of gold and fashioned with a seal bearing a picture of St. Peter fishing, surrounded by the new name by which the Pope chooses to be known. This ring is placed on his finger by the Cardinal Camerlengo, who removes it upon the death of the pontiff and destroys it by breaking it with a hammer.

In the Church of England, at the enthronement of a new British monarch, the Archbishop of Canterbury places a ring on the new king's or queen's right hand to remind them that they bear, among others, the title of Defender of the Faith.

Ornaments and Holy Things

Paschal Candle

Candles

Altar Candles

Advent Wreath

Advent Calendar

Creche

Bells

Paten

Holy Oil

Holy Water

Icons

PASCHAL CANDLE _____

In a completely darkened church on the Saturday night before Easter Day, the congregation waits in silence. The ministers are outside the nave, striking new fire. The fire is blessed and holy water is sprinkled on it. In the full ceremony the celebrant takes a large candle and carves on it a Greek cross, the Greek letters alpha and omega, and the calendar year in Arabic numerals. The celebrant inserts five grains of incense into the candle, symbolizing the five wounds of Christ. The celebrant then lights the candle from the new fire. The deacon takes the lit candle and leads the ministers into the darkened church. He stops three times and sings the "Lumen Christi"—The Light of Christ—in successively higher tones, to which the congregation responds, "Thanks be to God." The candle is then placed in its own candlestick, usually on the Gospel side of the altar, where the deacon chants the Exsultet, one of the most ancient hymns of the Christian Church. The other candles in the church are then lit from the flame of this candle.

This is the paschal candle. The word "pascha" comes from the Hebrew "pesach" which refers to the Passover. It connects us with the remembrance that Jesus is, for us, the Paschal Lamb. It also recalls the pillar of fire which led the people of Israel through the wilderness by night.

The use of lights (candles and lamps) in connection with the Easter Vigil dates from the 4th century. The striking of new fire arose in the Celtic Church and was known to St. Patrick. Until this century, the paschal candle was lit on Easter Eve and burned at all services until Ascension Day. Now it burns until the Day of Pentecost, which is the end of Eastertide.

The American Book of Common Prayer restored this ancient practice in the Proper Liturgy for the Great Vigil of Easter. In addition to its role in Easter, the paschal candle is used at baptism and burial. At Holy Baptism, a small candle is lit from the paschal candle, standing near the font, and handed to the newly baptized or the sponsors.

At a burial service the paschal candle may be carried into church before the body and placed near the coffin during the service.

The paschal candle burning through the Great Fifty Days of Easter is a witness to the presence of the Risen Christ on earth. The paschal candle burning at Holy Baptism symbolizes the Light of Christ which has triumphed over the forces of darkness in the world. The paschal candle burning at the Burial Office symbolizes the work of Christ in conquering death and reconciling humanity to God.

CANDLES

Burning candles are a symbol of joy and festivity both within and without the church, whether on an altar or a dining room table. Burning candles remind Christians that Jesus described himself as "the light of the world" (John 3:19, 8:12). The wax of the candle may symbolize the humanity of Christ and its flame his divinity. Lit candles remind Christians of the parable of the prudent virgins (Matthew 25:1-12) and may be a symbol of prayer and sacrifice.

Candles (or other burning lights) have been used in Christian worship since at least the 4th century. Presently, candles are used as processional torches, as Eucharistic lights or altar candles, as pavement lights, as candelabra, as the paschal candle, as baptismal candles, in an Advent wreath, in a sanctuary lamp, as votive lights and at special services such as Tenebrae.

Processional candles preceded the ministers into the church in the 4th century. These lights were placed around the altar and are the origin of both altar candles and pavement lights. Candles were first placed on Christian altars around the 11th century and became universal in the Middle Ages. Too much ado has been made about the correct number of altar candles. In most Episcopal churches, two candles are placed on the altar for use at the Holy Eucharist.

The use of the paschal candle at the Great Vigil of Easter and at Holy Baptism and burials is described in the American prayer book (pp. 285, 313, 467). Since the 12th century, a baptismal candle has been given to the newly baptized or to a godparent. This practice continues. The use of an Advent wreath is mentioned in the American prayer book (p. 143). A light which burns in many Episcopal (and Roman) sanctuaries signifies that the Blessed Sacrament is reserved. Votive lights are small candles, often in tiny glass containers, which are lit by individuals with prayer before icons or statues or side altars.

Tenebrae is an ancient liturgy, often scheduled during Lent and especially Holy Week, which involves the progressive extinguishing of candles. The Order of Worship for the Evening (BCP p. 109) contains numerous suggestions for the use of candles. Many Episcopal churches enjoy candlelight at Christmas Eve services in keeping with the birth of the Light of the World.

Only candles should be used where candles are called for, and these are traditionally of beeswax, if it can be afforded.

There is a tradition of blessing all of the candles to

be used in a year on Candlemas (the Feast of the Presentation, February 2).

ALTAR CANDLES _____

Candles, which once afforded practical illumination, now serve a decorative or symbolic function in churches. The use of candles on altars prompted a great controversy in the past.

As early Christian worship moved away from the Mediterranean and its abundant supply of olive oil for lamps, candles became the normative form of illumination around Christian altars. Until the 12th century, candles were carried in procession and then placed in holders near the altar, much as is now done with so-called pavement lights. By the late Middle Ages, candles had moved onto Christian altars where they have remained, more or less, ever since.

There has been considerable fuss over the appropriate number of candles to be placed on an altar. One 12th century source said two burned on the papal altar. Some English cathedrals (Chichester and Lincoln) used as many as seven in the pre-Reformation period at the same time when others (e.g. Durham) used only two. Archbishop Thomas Cranmer prescribed two for the altar in Canterbury Cathedral in 1547. Numerous 17th century prints show two candles on English altars and this number has come down to modern times as the norm. The Roman Church has made much of the use of the number of candles on the altar as an index of the importance of the occasion or the dignity of the celebrant or both.

No rubric in the American Episcopal Book of Common Prayer requires that candles be used on altars.

The rubrics in two services assume that such candles will be used. At the Great Vigil of Easter, a rubric (p. 294) directs when "the candles at the Altar" may be lit from the paschal candle. Likewise, in The Order of Worship for the Evening, a rubric (p. 112) directs that "candles at the Altar are now lighted."

Altar candles are normally white and made of beeswax. There is some tradition for using unbleached (yellowish) candles on Good Friday and at requiems. To the great distress of some people planning weddings, artificially colored candles are never used on the altar. While pink and purple candles may appear in an Advent wreath, they never make their way onto the altar.

Much used to be made of the order in which altar candles ought be lit and extinguished. Those on the Epistle side (to the right, when facing the altar from the nave) were always lit before those on the Gospel side and extinguished in reverse order. This is not part of prayer book liturgy and such things ought not take on the aspect of an epic production.

ADVENT WREATH _____

The evergreens of Christmastide are prefigured by a wreath of boughs surrounding four or five candles during the season of Advent. The Advent wreath probably came into popular Christian usage in the northern hemisphere from the Scandinavian Lutheran churches. Whatever its source, it has found a place not only in most American Episcopal churches but in the homes of many Episcopalians as well. The American Book of Common Prayer assumes that an Advent wreath is present in the church by giving instructions for its lighting during the Order of Worship for the Evening (p.

143). Forward Movement publishes a tract containing prayers and instructions for home Advent wreaths.

Advent wreaths are constructed with four candles arranged around a square or circle, each representing one of the Sundays in Advent. Sometimes a fifth candle—the Christ candle—is added to the center of the Advent wreath. Three of the four Advent candles are violet or purple, the liturgical color of Advent, and the fourth is sometimes rose. The Christ candle is always white.

One candle is lit on each Sunday of Advent, until all four candles are burning. The rose candle is lit on the Third Sunday of Advent. The Christ candle is lit on Christmas Eve. The number of candles burning thus tracks the progress of the season. Advent has long been observed with much of the penitential flavor of Lent— the use of purple vestments, omitting the Gloria in excelsis at Sunday celebrations of the Holy Eucharist. The Third Sunday of Advent—Gaudete Sunday—has been observed as a respite from the rigors of penitence, hence the use of rose-colored vestments and a rose candle in the Advent wreath. This is similar to the Fourth Sunday in Lent—Laetare Sunday—when again rose vestments are worn and the penitential observances of Lent are somewhat relaxed.

Advent comes at a time in the secular year when the days grow ever shorter and darkness falls a little earlier each day. Against this metaphor for the sinfulness of the world, the collect for the First Sunday of Advent prays "give us grace that—we may cast away the works of darkness, and put upon us the armor of light." These words are based on Romans 13:12. The flames in the Advent wreath can be for us a symbol of the coming of light into our lives which occurs when we "put on the Lord Jesus Christ" (Rom. 13:14). The lighting of the Christ candle on Christmas Eve can then be doubly celebrated as a symbol of Christ's Incarnation and as a symbol of his illumination of our lives.

ADVENT CALENDAR _____

It is human nature to "count the days" until some anticipated event. The prisoner counting the days until his release by marking his cell wall is a cartoon cliché. Members of the military create elaborate "short-time" calendars on which to reckon the days until discharge. Likewise expectant parents, children awaiting the last day of school or a birthday, and people of all ages who can hardly wait for Christmas.

This latter kind of counting the days often takes the form of a special calendar called an Advent calendar. Authorities differ as to the origin of Advent calendars; some say they originated in England, others in Sweden, still others in Germany.

The simplest Advent calendar is no more than a single page on which the typical box format of a monthly calendar is printed, the boxes of which can be checked off or covered by a sticker as each day before the Feast of the Nativity passes.

Next most elaborate are those Advent calendars which are made of two sheets of heavy paper with "doors" cut into the first sheet with something written, drawn or pasted inside each door. Each of these doors may conceal an appropriate seasonal picture or symbol, or a verse from Holy Scripture, or a reference to the proper lesson for the weekdays of Advent (see BCP pp. 936-39) which can then be read aloud, or an affirmation or word of encouragement from a book of daily affirmations, or an instruction concerning something to do or to avoid on that day, like a good deed or special devotion or a bit of self-denial.

Some imaginative people have made permanent Advent calendars out of wood. One enterprising design is composed of a pyramid of boxes.

Advent calendars, while especially popular with children and a good way to teach youngsters a bit about the sacred season, are not restricted to minors and may be enjoyed by grown-ups as well, most particularly those calendars which conceal a piece of foil-wrapped chocolate behind each door.

CRECHE

The use of a "creche" or manger scene at Christmas is a custom of the Western Church. Creche is an old French word for cradle, but has come to mean the complete scene of figures or models representing the first Christmas.

The inspiration for the Christmas creche is found in Luke 2:7—"She wrapped him in swaddling clothes, and laid him in a manger, because there was no room for them at the inn."

The first Christmas creche is attributed to St. Francis of Assisi who erected such a scene in Greccio in 1223. The Franciscan order sought to teach the Gospel to simple people through whatever means were available.

The medieval custom was to build a manger scene in the church, including statues of the Christ Child, the Blessed Virgin, St. Joseph, the shepherds and angels, and a variety of typical European barnyard animals. The figures of the Magi were not added until the Feast of the Epiphany on January 6.

The use of Christmas creches came under severe attack during the Protestant Reformation. Many opposed the use of all statuary because it violated the commandment against "graven images." In their zeal to cleanse the church, they destroyed many beautiful and historic creche figures, and the use of the creche waned in continental Europe.

However the creche never disappeared from English churches, maintained particularly by those parishes which kept many of the customs which the English Reformation sought to sweep away. Henry Cairncross, in his ritual written for English churches in the early 20th century, said: "It is a laudable and widespread custom at Christmas-tide to erect within our churches a representation of the birthplace of our blessed Redeemer."

An English ceremonial, published in the 1930s, contains many directions for the use of the Christmas creche. It is to be lit by two candles on sticks and never by artificial light. There must be a prayer desk located before the creche in order that the people may make their private devotions in visual contemplation of the scene. The creche must be blessed each year during the evening service on Christmas Eve.

BELLS

There are two sorts of liturgical bells in the history of the Christian Church—church bells in spires or towers used to call the faithful to worship, and sanctuary bells used to call attention to the coming of Christ in the Holy Eucharist.

Legend has it that Paulinus, the 5th century Bishop of Nola in Campania, first introduced church bells to

Christian worship. This legend explains the two Latin words for bells: nola and campana.

The use of church bells spread rapidly in the 6th century. It became customary to ring the church bells to call the faithful to worship and on other important occasions, such as the death of a parishioner. The 1552 English prayer book required that the church bell be rung to call the people to Morning and Evening Prayer. It is also traditional that the church bells ring during the processions of Candlemas (the Feast of the Purification) and Palm Sunday.

Since about the 8th century, church bells have been "baptized" with holy water and chrism, usually by a bishop. The bells were often named for saints and inscribed with dedications.

Smaller bells, often called sanctus bells, have long been rung in the sanctuary at the Sanctus, at the elevations of the elements, and to call the people forward to the communion.

It is traditional that no bells be rung from the last service on Maundy Thursday until the Great Vigil of Easter. There is no Anglican authority for the tolling of church bells at 3 p.m. on Good Friday to mark Jesus' giving up the spirit, but it is done in some places.

In the medieval liturgies, every bell in the church was rung during the Gloria in excelsis on the Great Vigil of Easter. This remains the Episcopal tradition.

From about the 15th century, church bells have been rung at early morning, noon and around 6 p.m. to call the Roman Catholic faithful to say the Angelus—three Hail Marys and a collect—in honor of the Incarnation. The bell is sometimes rung a fourth time, an hour after the last Angelus, to call the faithful to pray for the departed by saying Psalm 130, the De Profundis.

The voices of church bells speak to mourning, to

devotion to the Blessed Sacrament, to the call to prayer, and to occasions of great joy.

PATEN

A paten is a (usually) circular (usually) metal plate on which the eucharistic bread is placed during the Great Thanksgiving (the prayer of consecration) and the distribution of the elements. The term "paten" is from the Middle English, derived from an Old French word, "patene," which was probably derived from the Latin "patina" meaning "a pan." Patens are often curved up at the outer edges, in order to more safely contain wafer bread, giving them a resemblance to pans.

In the early Church, patens were large enough to hold an entire round loaf of home-baked bread, brought by a member of the congregation to the Eucharist. Over time, especially in the Western Church, patens grew smaller and smaller as the use of wafer bread replaced loaves. A typical modern paten is only six to seven inches in diameter.

From about the 10th century, patens were partially replaced in some places by a metal cup (resembling a chalice with a lid) called a ciborium. This vessel was less likely to allow consecrated hosts to drop to the floor during administration than was the paten (on which the priest's host might still be consecrated).

A typical medieval paten was made of silver or gold. Puritan clergy sought to identify the Eucharist with an ordinary meal; thus they favored the use of pewter goblets and plates. Revival of traditional practice restored the use of silver and gold as the most common materials for chalice and paten. Alternative modern materials include cut crystal, wood, pottery and virtually any other serviceable medium.

Modern patens are usually part of a communion set and match the chalice in materials and design. It is also common for a paten in a set to be so designed as to "nest" atop the chalice, the better to stack them in preparation for the celebration.

In the Eastern Church, the equivalent of the paten is called a "diskos." This is normally larger than the western paten and may be made with a pedestal or foot.

Some hold that sacred vessels are consecrated by being used for the purpose for which they were made. Others hold that such objects ought be blessed before use. Adherents to the latter school also tend to hold that only a bishop may bless a paten.

Often a newly-ordained priest is both vested in chasuble and invested with a paten and chalice immediately after the prayer consecrating him or her.

HOLY OIL

Olive oil figures significantly in the Old Testament. It was an important dietary element (1 Kings 17:12-16). It was mixed with aromatics to make perfumes (Esther 2:12; Song of Songs 1:3; 4:10). It was understood as a symbol of refreshment and happiness (Psalms 23:5; 104:15). It was used in the purification of healed lepers by anointing the right ear, thumb and toe (Lev. 14). It was also used to consecrate kings, priests and (sometimes) prophets. The recipe for the oil used to anoint priests survives in Exodus 30:22-25. A common 1st century Jewish practice was to pray for sick persons and to anoint them with oil (James 5:14).

The early Church derived its uses of oil from Jewish practice. Three sorts of oils were widely used: oil for exorcism, for baptism and for healing. From the 2nd century, catechumens were anointed with the oil of exorcism as part of their preparation to receive baptism at the Great Vigil of Easter. Immediately upon coming up from the waters of baptism, they were again anointed with a different oil called "chrism" or the oil of thanksgiving. "Chrism" derives from the Greek verb "to anoint"; the title "Christ" means "anointed." The oil for the sick, also known as the oil of gladness, was used to anoint those who were ill.

There are numerous mentions of these oils in the Early Fathers of the Church. From the 4th century until the present the consecration of holy oil was reserved for bishops. The American prayer book provides for a priest to bless oil for healing (p. 455). Since the 8th century, the practice of the Western Church has been for the bishop to consecrate chrism for use throughout his diocese on Maundy Thursday. In the rites of Salisbury Cathedral before the Reformation, the bishop consecrated all three oils on Maundy Thursday.

The use of chrism was rejected by the protestants as having no foundation in Holy Scripture. Chrismation at baptism was included in the 1549 English prayer book but dropped from the 1552. Similarly, the anointing of the sick was part of the 1549 prayer book but omitted from the 1552. Anointing of the sick was restored to the American prayer book of 1928 and anointing of the baptized was restored to the American prayer book of 1979.

In the 1979 prayer book, chrismation (using oil blessed by a bishop on his visitation) occurs at Holy Baptism (p. 308). In some dioceses, a chrism service is celebrated by the bishop on Maundy Thursday. A form of anointing of the sick is also provided (BCP pp. 455-457). In the form for celebrating a new ministry, one of the gifts given to the new rector or vicar is holy oil (p. 561).

HOLY WATER

Water is a powerful symbol and metaphor in Judeo-Christian experience. God led the people of Israel through parted waters of the Red Sea and then gave them water to drink from the rock in the wilderness. Jesus began his earthly ministry after baptism in the waters of the Jordan River. He offered the Samaritan woman at the well "living water." The water in the pool at Bethesda was believed to be stirred by an angel and to have curative properties. The Church Fathers saw all these as metaphors for the water of baptism.

The Early Church used water in both sacramental and ceremonial ways. When Rome became Christian, public buildings which had been used as pagan temples were sprinkled with water as part of their consecration for Christian worship. From the 5th century the sick were sprinkled with water as part of the ministry of healing. In medieval times, mothers were sprinkled with holy water after the birth of their children. In pre-Reformation England, the palms were sprinkled with holy water before the procession on Palm Sunday and the paschal candle was sprinkled with holy water at the Great Vigil of Easter.

English churches built from Norman times until the English Reformation normally had holy water stoups located near the main door. The common practice was to take holy water upon entering and leaving the church as a reminder of one's baptism. The manner of "taking" holy water is to dip the middle finger of the right hand into the water, touch it to the forehead and then make the sign of the cross. This practice has been revived in the modern English Church and, to a lesser extent, in the Episcopal.

In 1536, Archbishop Thomas Cranmer, although opposed to many Roman practices, encouraged the sprinkling of holy water, along with such practices as the imposition of ashes on Ash Wednesday and the carrying of palms on Palm Sunday.

In the modern Roman Catholic Church, holy water is sprinkled on the people during the entrance of the ministers at the Mass. This is called the "asperges," after the first word of Psalm 51 in Latin, "Asperges me, Domine," used as an anthem during the ritual. The English Church has practiced the asperges since the 9th century. The most common use of it in the Episcopal Church is after the renewal of baptismal vows at the Easter Vigil, Pentecost Day, All Saints' Day and the First Sunday after the Epiphany.

In some parts of the church, the faithful take home small bottles of holy water, blessed at the Easter Vigil, for private use, especially at times of illness.

The magical or superstitious use of holy water, often depicted in movies, has given a bad name to a holy practice which is only slowly being restored to its proper and historic position.

ICONS

Upon entering an Eastern Orthodox Church, one's eye is quickly drawn to the many stylized paintings hung both on the iconostasis (the screen separating the nave from the sanctuary) and on the surrounding walls.

Icons are flat paintings, originally of egg tempera on wood, but now made of many modern materials. These icons typically depict Christ, the Blessed Virgin

(Theotokos), biblical figures and other saints.

The likenesses do not seek to reproduce photographic reality. Rather they follow ancient traditional norms for the depiction of holy persons. Every detail of the icon has meaning, including the backgrounds and all the small details.

The widespread use of icons in the Eastern Church dates from at least the 5th century and was only increased by the iconoclastic controversy of the 8th and 9th centuries. For various reasons, the use of icons was banned by Emperor Leo III in 726, which set off a controversy lasting over a hundred years. The devotion of the Eastern monks to their icons was so fierce that many died defending them against military persons ordered to destroy them. "Iconoclast" is a Greek word meaning "image breaker." The controversy ended in 843 but left one of the major scars responsible for the separation of the Eastern and Western Churches in 1054.

Icons are highly venerated in the modern Orthodox Church. In both public and private devotions of the Orthodox, they play a major role. Because of the second commandment's injunction against the worship of any object, Orthodox theologians argue that worship and veneration are not the same thing. The Orthodox understand and defend the use of icons as a sacramental way of seeing through the painting and through the figure depicted to the God who lies behind and on the other side of human reality. In this sense, an icon is more like a lens which focuses spiritual sight than a figure which is perceived by seeing.

All interest in artistic depictions of biblical figures and of other saints was condemned by most of the leaders of the Protestant Reformation, e.g. John Calvin and Ulrich Zwingli, although Martin Luther permitted the use of the crucifix.

Anglican interest in icons dates from the affinity of the 16th century reformers of the Church of England to the spirituality of the Eastern Church, which is reflected in some of the liturgies in the 1549 English prayer book. Anglicans have tended neither to oppose religious art with the zeal of the early protestants nor to embrace it with the zeal of the Orthodox for their icons.

Worship Traditions

Kneeling

Bowing

Genuflection

Lavabo

Stripping the Altar

KNEELING _____

In the Old Testament, kneeling was a posture of prayer. King Solomon knelt to pray (1 Kings 8:54; 2 Chronicles 6:13); likewise Ezra (Ezra 9:5) and Daniel (Daniel 6:10). Kneeling was a posture of submission to God (Isaiah 45:23; Romans 14:11) or to a false god (1 Kings 19:18). Old Testament people knelt before those whom they acknowledged as a master, e.g. Elijah (2 Kings 1:13). Hence Psalm 95:6, "Come, let us bow down, and bend the knee, and kneel before the Lord our Maker."

In the New Testament, people continued to kneel to pray, e.g. Stephen (Acts 7:60), Peter (Acts 9:40), Luke (Acts 21:5) and Paul (Acts 20:36; Ephesians 3:14). These early Christians followed the example of Jesus, who knelt to pray to his Father (Luke 22:41). In the New Testament, people knelt before Jesus when they acknowledged him as their master (e.g. Matthew 8:2; 9:18; 15:25; 17:14; 20:20).

There is evidence that people in the early church both stood and knelt to pray in congregational worship.

Congregational kneeling became the norm in the medieval church because the people were left to their own private prayer during the liturgy and the posture of kneeling seemed appropriate. Kneeling to receive Holy Communion was also the norm at the time of the English Reformation. There was fierce Puritan opposition to this practice on the grounds that it accorded too much deference to mere things, e.g. the bread and wine. The American prayer book provides no directions as to the proper posture for receiving Holy Communion. The piety which requires kneeling remains part of American Episcopal custom, expressed by Hymn 325, "Let us break bread together on our knees."

The old direction, "kneel to pray, stand to praise

and sit to listen," was never entirely reliable as a direction for Episcopal posture in worship. An old English canon directed that during prayer "all manner of persons then present shall reverently kneel upon their knees." English liturgist Percy Dearmer counseled "When in doubt as to the attitude for prayer, let the priest stand and the people kneel."

The American Book of Common Prayer provides very few rubrics which direct the posture of priest or people. This silence permits great flexibility in local and/or seasonal usages. People who normally kneel to receive communion are free to stand during the Great Fifty Days of Easter or when the sacrament is distributed at stations.

Kneeling continues to express humility and penitence. Thus the confession of sin is said kneeling in both the Daily Office and the Holy Eucharist. The Great Litany may be sung or said "kneeling, standing or in procession," there being historical warrant for all three.

BOWING

Saint Paul says that Christ was exalted in heaven and that, at the Name of Jesus, every knee should bow. (Phil. 2:10) The earliest Christians took this injunction literally and followed the practice of bowing whenever the Name of Jesus was spoken aloud. The English practice has always been the same; the canons of 1603 and 1640 both required that church members bow at the Name of Jesus, not only when it is mentioned in the Creed but at all times during the service. This practice explains the 18th century hymn, "The God of Abraham praise" (401, Hymnal 1982) which says, "We bow and bless the sacred Name."

Bowing in the church has taken various forms and found various occasions. One commentator identifies three kinds of liturgical bows: profound, moderate and simple. The profound bow is made from the waist. The moderate bow is of the head and shoulders (sort of like looking at one's feet). The simple bow is the bending of the head only. The occasions for bowing are numerous.

Throughout the church and its history, the faithful have bowed to the altar. There was never the sense that the altar itself was being worshiped; the reverence is to the presence of the Divine Majesty which the altar symbolizes. For example, canon 7 of 1640 requires that the people bow to the altar "both at their coming in and their going out of . . . churches." The same piety explains the practice of bowing to the altar upon entering and leaving the pew, and upon approaching and leaving the altar at Holy Communion.

Despite considerable protestant opposition, numerous other occasions for bowing remain part of Anglican worship. Members of the congregation bow as the processional cross passes by them. Many bow their heads at the mention of the Holy Trinity (as in the Gloria Patri); this practice dates back at least to 1305 in England and 1351 in Ireland. When incense is used, a deep bow is exchanged between the thurifer and the persons being censed. The people bow toward the Book of the Gospel during the Gloria tibi ("Glory be to thee . . .") and the Laus tibi ("Praise be to thee . . ."). The people bow during the words describing the Incarnation in the creed.

Ministers occasionally bow to each other—the priest and the server, after the celebrant washes his hands; the oblation bearers and the acolyte, when the offering is presented at the altar.

Bowing can be empty ritual or it can engage the mind and body of the worshiper at once in acts of profound devotion. It need not be practiced by everyone; those who are physically incapable of or psychologically uncomfortable with bowing should refrain. Others are encouraged to join in the practice of the church in saying with their bodies what their minds and lips say with their prayers.

GENUFLECTION

There is a hymn of the ancient church which was either written or quoted by St. Paul in Philippians 2:9-11. A verse of it says, "At the name of Jesus every knee should bend . . . and every tongue should confess that Jesus Christ is Lord." This verse inspired two hymns in the American Episcopal Church's Hymnal 1982. The first verse of Hymn 435 proclaims, "At the Name of Jesus, every knee shall bow, every tongue confess him, King of glory now." The fourth verse of Hymn 60 begins, "At your great Name, O Jesus, now all knees must bend, all hearts must bow."

The term genuflection is derived from a compound of two Latin words: "genu" meaning "knee" and "flectere" meaning "to bend." An alternate English spelling is genuflexion.

The dictionary definition of the term is a bending of one knee as a sign of reverence during worship. The practice is common only in the Western Church where the form of genuflection is to kneel on the right knee while bending the left knee somewhat, all the while holding the body erect. Sometimes the posture of kneeling on both knees with the head bowed is called a double genuflection.

Genuflection is normally associated with the sacrament of Holy Eucharist. It may be seen done by persons entering or leaving the nave of a church in which the Blessed Sacrament is reserved, or by those crossing in front of the Reserved Sacrament, or by those who are entering or leaving a pew, or during the words describing the Incarnation in the Nicene Creed. While there is evidence of genuflection in the 14th and 15th centuries, it became standardized in the reformed Roman mass of the 16th century. Just as the Puritans were opposed to kneeling while receiving the Holy Communion, so they were opposed to genuflection.

The Anglican liturgist Percy Dearmer was thoroughly opposed to genuflection, which he referred to as "that practice of dropping to one knee." Part of the debate in Anglican churches arises from the definition of the word "genuflexio" in ancient ceremonials: whether it means genuflection as understood modernly (the Roman Catholic position) or means simply kneeling (Dearmer's position).

Local policy should determine when and if the vested ministers genuflect during the liturgy. As an act of private devotion, it is appropriate for those who find it both physically comfortable and spiritually meaningful. In no sense should genuflection become a statement of allegiance to some branch or party within the church.

LAVABO

It must appear strange to the uninitiated when the celebrant at Holy Eucharist pauses between the Offertory and the Eucharistic Prayer and washes his hands. The practice, known as the Lavabo, is of great antiquity and serves practical as well as spiritual ends.

There is an ancient tradition of ministers washing their hands before vesting, which was largely practical (to keep the vestments clean). The first mention of the celebrant washing hands before the consecration is found in the 4th century. This is described as an act of piety, symbolic of the cleansing of one's self before approaching the altar of God.

The ceremony may derive in part from the Old Testament where the Jewish priests were required to wash their hands before going into the Tent of the Presence or approaching the altar to make a sacrifice (Exodus 30:19-21). Or it may derive from the first century Jewish practice of ritual hand-washing before meals. St. Mark explains that the Jews always washed their hands before eating, in obedience to a long-established tradition (Mark 7:3-4).

Some authorities believe that the practice arose during that ancient time when the celebrants received all sorts of gifts at the offertory and needed to wash their hands before the consecration.

The ceremony normally involves the celebrant stepping near the credence table. A deacon or acolyte holds a lavabo bowl in one hand and a cruet of water in the other. The server pours the water over the celebrant's hands so that it falls into the bowl. The celebrant then takes a towel from the server's wrist, dries his hands, and returns it.

Some priests say a portion of Psalm 26:6 during this ceremony: "I will wash my hands in innocence . . ." The name lavabo comes from the first word of this passage in Latin: "Lavabo inter innocentes." The Roman ritual appointed Psalm 26:6 for use during this ceremony until 1969 when it adopted part of Psalm 51 in its place. Howard Galley's Episcopal ceremonial manual recommends Psalm 51:11 for use during the lavabo: "Create in me a clean heart, O God, and renew a right spirit within me."

This ceremony is mentioned in the pre-reformation missals of York, Salisbury (Sarum), and Hereford Cathedrals. Some English church manuals call it "the lavatory" which carries an unfortunate connotation in modern American usage.

Marion Hatchett, in his manual of ceremonial for the 1979 American Book of Common Prayer, suggests that the ministers who will handle the elements wash their hands before the eucharistic prayer. His suggestion includes those ministers other than the celebrant who will distribute communion.

STRIPPING THE ALTAR

The Proper Liturgy for Maundy Thursday in the American Book of Common Prayer (pp. 274-5) says nothing whatsoever about stripping and washing the altar at the conclusion of the Holy Eucharist on this night. This ancient ceremony is nonetheless enacted in many Episcopal churches.

The practice is over a thousand years old. In the 8th century Gallican Church the altars were stripped and washed on Good Friday. This was done on Maundy Thursday in Rome. At Salisbury Cathedral in the Middle Ages, the clergy first celebrated the mass on Maundy Thursday and then left the church for refreshments. Upon returning they stripped and washed the altars, after which they retired to the chapter house for the washing of feet.

The American Book of Occasional Services mentions the "Stripping of the Altar" on Maundy Thursday and suggests that it be done upon the completion of the proper liturgy. The rubrics permit this to be done as a public or private ceremony. It may be done in silence or accompanied by the recitation of Psalm 22. If Psalm 22 is used, an antiphon is provided: "They divide my garments among them; they cast lots for my clothing."

There is a great diversity of practice in the performance of this ceremony. Generally, the ministers leave the sanctuary at the conclusion of the Holy Eucharist and remove their outer vestments of white. They then return in either plain girded albs or in albs with purple stoles. Some manuals direct only that everything be removed from the altar; others direct that the altar be washed.

The ministers remove the altar cross, the candlesticks and any other objects on the altar. Then the altar hangings are removed. If there are multiple altars in the church, the high altar is stripped first and then the others. The high altar is left bare and the tabernacle empty and open.

If the altar is to be washed, after it is stripped it is customary to pour a little wine on each of the five crosses incised in its surface. Water is then used to wash the entire surface. It is an English custom to dry the surface with a branch of boxwood or other tree branch.

The stripping and washing of the altar has both utilitarian and symbolic functions. It is part of the "spring cleaning" of the church in anticipation of the Queen of Feasts. It recalls that our Lord was stripped of his garments during his torment. It prepares the altar for the stark services of Good Friday. It prepares the faithful for the sobriety of recalling the Death of God before the joy of celebrating his Resurrection.

Symbols

THE POWER OF SYMBOLS _____

Symbols are capable of expressing things which empirical terms are not. To know the chemical formula for a perfume or a fine wine is not to know all there is to know about it. Laboratory analysis can describe things in one way but poetry, metaphor, images, and music can say things which science cannot.

Symbols measure things which cannot otherwise be measured. There is no sense to a quart of love, or a furlong of beauty or a nanosecond of truth. While we can say descriptive things about love, beauty and truth in empirical-sounding words, they are best described symbolically.

A flower pressed in a scrapbook may say more about a first date with a lover than all of the descriptions possible—elapsed time, geographical location in longitude and latitude, ambient air temperature, and so on.

Symbols are not true in the same way as other statements. That one hundred pennies make a dollar is true. That Jesus Christ was the Lamb of God is also true. Each of these is subject to verification, one by calculation and law, the other by inspiration and faith.

It is a foolish person who attempts to kidnap a symbol from its proper realm and transport it into the realm of literal truth. Thus when one says that "my love is like a red, red rose," it is foolish to inquire if the beloved has thorns and petals. To remain sensible, the symbol must remain in its proper frame.

The modern mind rebels against the unknowable. Thus we use microscopes and telescopes to see what the unaided eye cannot. We use computers to count what we cannot count on our fingers and toes. We climb to the top and dive to the bottom to see what is there. When faced with the truly unknowable, we resort to symbols.

God is unknowable, and truth about God must be expressed in symbolic language. It makes no sense to ask the size or weight (or age) of God, just as it makes no sense to ask what is the meaning of sodium chloride. When Jesus spoke of the Kingdom of Heaven, he frequently resorted to symbols—a mustard seed, a pearl, a buried treasure.

To be a Christian is to live in a world filled with symbols in scripture, art, music, architecture, liturgy and prayer. Just as an immigrant must learn to speak the language of her adopted country, so the Christian must learn the language of the symbols which abound in the Church.

SYMBOLS OF THE TRINITY ____

The doctrine of the Holy Trinity is easy to say but hard to understand. The Athansian Creed says, "That we worship one God in Trinity, and Trinity in Unity, neither confounding the Persons, nor dividing the Substance." The Thirty Nine Articles say, "There is but one living and true God . . . and in the Unity of this Godhead there be three Persons, of one substance, power, and eternity: the Father, the Son, and the Holy Ghost." The Church often resorts to symbols to say better what words cannot say well.

Probably the oldest symbols depicting the Holy Trinity are triangles, especially equilateral triangles, sometimes in elaborate forms. Another early symbol is of three fishes, each with its head at the tail of another, forming a circle or triangle.

Natural symbols were also used by the early Church to teach the doctrine of the Trinity. These include the triple leaf of the anemone and the three-petaled fleurde-lis. Legend has it that St. Patrick used the sham-rock, similar in appearance to a three-leaf clover, to teach the doctrine to the pagans of Ireland.

A shield of the doctrine of the Blessed Trinity, used by early armorists, also appears on the banners of some churches dedicated to the Trinity. It is composed of three circles arranged around a central fourth. In the center circle is written "Deus"—God. In each outer circle is written either "Pater," "Filius," or "Spiritus"—Father, Son, or Spirit. Each of the outer circles is connected to the adjacent circles with a banner reading "non est"— is not. Each of the outer circles in connected to the inner circle with a banner reading "est"—is.

During the Renaissance, painters represented the Trinity with a white-bearded old man standing behind a younger Jesus, on or holding the cross, with the Holy Spirit shown as a white dove at the foot of the cross. In this same period, the Trinity was also symbolized by an eye within a triangle with rays shining out in three directions, probably derived from Proverbs 15:3.

The words "Sanctus" or "Holy" repeated thrice rep-resent the Trinity. This derives from both Isaiah 6:3 and Revelation 4:8. The familiar hymn "Holy, Holy, Holy" (362, Hymnal 1982) is an example.

If the unity of God is being emphasized, a single symbol is used. If the persons within the Holy Trinity are being emphasized, a depiction of three objects or persons is preferred. While both are true, both are in error. This is because the Holy Trinity is a Holy Mys-tery. As Isaac Watts says, in Hymn 369, "Our reason stretches all its wings and climbs above the skies; but still how far beneath thy feet our groundling knowl-edge lies!"

ALPHA AND OMEGA _____

Some concepts are so difficult to grasp in concrete terms that they are better expressed symbolically. Certainly one such concept is the infinitude of God. Temporally, God was before anything else was and will be long after everything else is not.

The early Christians used the Greek letters alpha and omega in conjunction to express this notion. Because alpha is the first and omega is the last letter of the Greek alphabet, they were probably used colloquially in the 1st century to stand for "the beginning and the end," much as a modern retail establishment might advertise that it has "everything from A to Z." Early Christians understood the letters to connote "from the beginning of all things to the end of all things" or "from creation to the eschaton." When used to describe God, alpha and omega implied "more than all" in the sense that God transcends both the beginning and the end of time.

This idea appears in the Old Testament (Isaiah 44:6) where God is described as "the first" and "the last." St. John employs the idea and the symbol three times in Revelation—in 1:8 and 21:6 to describe "the Lord God" and in 22:13 to describe Jesus Christ.

When the Greek letters alpha and omega are seen together on a crest or shield or on the pages of an open book in Renaissance art, they refer to Christ and derive from Revelation 22:13. Likewise in Christian heraldry, alpha and omega are used as a device signifying Christ.

One of the emphases of the season of Advent is "first and last things," thus the alpha and omega are appropriate symbols for this season and are frequently used in liturgical art (banners, bulletin covers, stoles). In this sense, they refer to Christ as the pre-existent creator of all things and to Christ as the one whose Second Coming will conclude all things.

Alpha and omega are also part of the Christmas liturgy, when the 4th century hymn "Of the Father's love begotten" (82, Hymnal 1982) is sung. Its first verse describes Christ as both the source and the ending of all that was and is and will be.

Sung in every season, the 7th century eucharistic hymn "Draw nigh and take the Body of the Lord" concludes with a reference to Christ as "Alpha-Omega." (327-8, v. 8, Hymnal 1982)

The Christian use of alpha and omega is in some sense related to the Jewish use of the word "emet." This word means "truth" and is composed of the first and last letters of the Hebrew alphabet. It is used in Jewish symbolism in roughly the same manner in which Christians use alpha and omega.

INSTRUMENTS
OF THE PASSION _____

Nothing in all human history has inspired more artistic effort than the depiction of the Passion of our Lord. Included within the Passion are his betrayal, his trial, abuse at the hands of Roman soldiers, and his crucifixion. Appreciation of the many works of art concerning these subjects requires an understanding of the symbols which have become associated with the Passion.

Depictions of the betrayal of Jesus often include coins and/or a purse, torches, and a cock or rooster. Judas betrayed Jesus for thirty pieces of silver. Coins

scattered on the ground represent his attempt to return the blood money. The purse is a symbol of this
money and of Judas' role as treasurer of the Disciples.
Jesus was arrested at night; the torch has thus been
used as a symbol of betrayal as well. The cock symbolizes Peter's denial of Jesus before the cock crew—a
Jewish colloquialism for early morning.

Depictions of the trial and abuse of Jesus often include a basin and pitcher, a robe, crown of thorns and
reed, and a column and scourges. The basin and pitcher
refer to Pilate's attempt to rid himself of guilt in the
death of Jesus by washing his hands. The soldiers, who
taunted Jesus as a false king, dressed him in a purple
robe, placed a crown of thorns on his head and gave
him a reed for a scepter. The crown of thorns was a
parody of the Roman emperor's crown of roses. Jesus
was likely bound to a column by the soldiers who
whipped him with a scourge—a short whip made of multiple cords. A pillar with loosed cords at its base stands
for the beating given to Jesus.

Depictions of the crucifixion often include hammer
and nails, dice, a reed and a sponge, a spear, a skull
and a ladder. The holes in Jesus' hands, which he
showed to the Disciples, are signified by the hammer
and nails. The soldiers cast lots for Jesus' garments;
dice shown on a cloak symbolize this. A sponge on the
end of a reed was used to offer sour wine to Jesus while
he was on the cross. A spear was used to pierce Jesus'
side. It is sometimes shown crossed with the reed. A
skull and other bones may be pictured at the foot of
the cross because Golgotha—the place of the crucifixion—means "place of the skull." Legend has it that the
cross was raised over Adam's tomb, thus the skull and
bones are to be thought of as his. While no ladder is
mentioned in scripture, medieval artists assumed that

one was used by Nicodemus and Joseph of Arimathea to remove Jesus' body.

INRI

The Gospel According to St. John provides the most complete account of a sign posted on the cross when Jesus was crucified. It was, according to John, written by Pontius Pilate and contained the words "Jesus of Nazareth, the King of the Jews" in three languages—Latin, Hebrew and Greek. This account (John 19:19-20) is contained in the Passion Gospel traditionally read on Good Friday.

The Synoptic Gospels' accounts of the Crucifixion, those read on Palm Sunday in successive years, provide different details about this sign. Matthew 27:37 says that it was placed over Jesus' head and read "This is Jesus, the King of the Jews." Matthew calls the sign the "charge" against Jesus and does not say who wrote it. Mark 15:26 says that there was an inscription (without saying where it was placed nor by whom it was written) which stated the "charge against him" and read "The King of the Jews." Luke 23:38 indicates that an inscription was placed "over him" reading "This is the King of the Jews."

Because two of the Gospel accounts (Matthew and Luke) say that the writing was placed over Jesus' head, it is often referred to as "the superscription," which simply means "the writing above."

Only John identifies the languages in which the superscription was written. A few manuscripts of John's Gospel change the word "Hebrew" to "Aramaic." Passersby would have been able to read one of these languages, if they were able to read at all, and John may mention this detail in order to underscore the universality of Jesus' mission.

Early Christian depictions of the Crucifixion show the entire text of the superscription. Later depictions use the full text but in only one language—that most likely understood by the artist's audience. The Latin version read "Iesus Nazarenus Rex Iudaeorum." From the 13th century, Italian painters abbreviated the inscription to its initials in Latin: INRI.

Numerous examples of this abbreviated superscription appear in Renaissance painting, such as Francesco del Cossa's "The Crucifixion," Guidoccio Cozzarelli's "The Crucifixion," and Francesco Pesellino's "The Crucifixion with Saint Jerome and Saint Francis."

The initials INRI frequently appear in sacred art, vestments, paraments, banners and the like, often in connection with Holy Week.

God often reverses things: the weak are made strong, the small become great and, in the case of INRI, a mockery becomes a symbol of the real kingship of Jesus Christ.

PALM

The earliest use of palm branches, found in the Old Testament, is in connection with the Feast of Tabernacles. Leviticus 23:39-44 decrees a harvest festival during which the people are to construct arbors or booths (tabernacles) of the branches of citrus, willow (or poplar) and palm, and live in them for seven days.

The palm was also a Roman symbol of military victory. Legions would return from a successful campaign carrying palm branches as a symbol of their conquest. The Jewish celebration of the recapture of Jerusalem and the purification of the Temple by Judas Maccabaeus is recorded in 2 Maccabees 10:7 and included the use of palms.

This symbolism of victory, sometimes adopted by Jews, illuminates the peoples' use of palm branches at Jesus' triumphal entry into Jerusalem, which is described in John 12:12-14.

Another use of the palm is as a symbol of spiritual victory or of victory over death. This association derives, in part, from the vision of heaven described in Revelation 7:9 in which John sees a huge crowd of people, dressed in white, standing around the throne and the Lamb, each carrying a palm branch.

In sacred art, the palm branch is most often a symbol of the martyr's triumph over physical death. In heraldry, the shield of a martyr is often composed of the instrument of death and of a palm branch. For example, the shield of St. Stephen, the first Christian martyr, is composed of three stones and a palm branch. Icons of the 3rd century St. Euphemia, a popular martyr in the Greek Church, always show her holding a palm branch as a symbol of her beheading. Whenever a saint is depicted in a medieval painting as holding a palm, this is most likely a symbol of martyrdom.

The legend of St. Christopher holds that he uprooted a young palm tree and used it as a walking stick to steady himself while he carried the Christ Child across a river. The legend continues that he thrust the palm tree back into the ground on the far side of the river, whereupon it promptly took root, blossomed and bore fruit.

Palms have been used liturgically in the Church since earliest times. The writings of Egeria, a nun who visited the Holy Land in the late 4th century, describe a Holy Week procession to the Mount of Olives in

Jerusalem in which the faithful carry palms. This use continues in the modern Church. The ashes imposed on Ash Wednesday are traditionally made by burning the palms used on the previous Palm Sunday.

DOVE

The first Old Testament reference to a dove is in the story of Noah releasing a dove from the ark to discover when the waters had safely retreated (Genesis 8:8-12). Doves were common in Palestine and were among the animals sacrificed in the Temple at Jerusalem in Jesus' day (Matthew 21:12; Mark 11:14; John 2:16).

Because of its perceived traits, a dove is used metaphorically in Holy Scripture to represent innocence (Matthew 10:16), silliness (Hosea 7:11), the ability to fly (Psalm 55:6; Isaiah 60:8), moaning (Isaiah 38:14, 59:11; Ezekiel 7:16; Nahum 2:7), fearfulness (Hosea 11:11), and a beautiful woman (Song of Songs 2:14, 5:2, 6:9).

For Christians, the most important reference to a dove in Holy Scripture occurs in connection with John's baptism of Jesus in the River Jordan. Jesus' favor with the Father was manifested by the descent of the Holy Spirit upon him in the form of a dove (Matthew 3:16; Mark 1:10; Luke 3:22; John 1:32).

It is because of this latter reference that the dove usually represents the Holy Spirit in Christian art. The symbolism from the Old Testament nonetheless is still used. The white dove with an olive branch in its mouth is a symbol of peace, relating to the Flood Story in Genesis. Christian interpreters identified the bride in the Song of Songs with the Church—the bride of Christ; thus the Church is sometimes represented by a dove.

Because St. Benedict had a vision of a dove rising

before he was told of the death of his sister, St. Scholastica, his shield often bears a dove ascending. St. David of Wales was unable to be heard by a large assembly of Welsh bishops until a dove perched on his shoulder, hence the dove sometimes seen on his crest. St. Gregory is similarly depicted in Renaissance art with a dove on his shoulder, based on the legend that the Holy Spirit whispered to him the words upon which his writings were based.

A eucharistic dove is a hollow sculpture of a dove used to hold the Reserved Sacrament which was sometimes "flown" over the altar by suspending it from fine chain. Such usages date from the 11th century, were common in medieval England, but are now rare.

Numerous hymns in the Hymnal 1982 refer to doves, particularly in connection with the Baptism of our Lord (120, 121), with God the Holy Spirit (371, 509, 510, 512, 513, 683), and as a symbol of peace (399). A well-accepted addition to the hymnal is "Like the murmur of the dove's song," words by Carl P. Daw Jr.

ROCK

Many old Testament symbols are derived from nature. David is represented by a lion's head, Noah by a dove with an olive sprig, Jonah by a whale, Passover by a lamb, Pentecost by a sheaf of wheat and so on. It is not surprising that rock was used as a symbol for the Lord God because of its weighty and enduring qualities. This association was bolstered by the story of Moses striking the rock at Horeb, from which the Lord provided water for the children of Israel (Exodus 17:6; Numbers 20:8-12; Psalm 105:41; Isaiah 48:21). As a result, God is frequently referred to in the Old

Testament as "my rock," "the rock of salvation," or "the rock of Israel" (Deut. 32:15; 2 Sam. 22:2; Psalms 18:2, 42:9, 62:2, 6; Isaiah 26:4; Habakkuk 1:12.)

In 1 Corinthians, Paul suggests that Jesus was the rock at Horeb (10:4), recalling a Jewish legend which held that the rock followed Israel through the desert. To Paul, this rock was the pre-existent Christ.

Jesus said of St. Peter, "On this rock will I build my church." (Matthew 16:18) The name Peter derives from the Greek "Petra" which means rock.

Rock, in Renaissance painting, is often a symbol of the Divine Presence. Such rocks, usually massive, are not to be confused with the stones which sometimes symbolize St. Stephen or St. Timothy, both of whom were martyred by stoning.

Probably the best known rock image for God is in the hymn "Rock of Ages" (685, Hymnal 1982). This hymn was written by an English vicar, the Rev. Augustus Montague Toplady (1740-1778). Just three years before his death, Toplady was walking on the road to Cheddar when a sudden storm drove him to the shelter of a cleft running down a rock ledge beside the road. In this shelter, he found a playing card, the six of diamonds, and wrote the entire first verse of the hymn on its reverse. The personal quality of this hymn is attributable to Toplady's evangelical sympathies. He was educated at Trinity College in Dublin, and ordained in the Church of England but served at the French Calvinist Chapel in London. The rock which inspired his hymn can be visited today in Burrington Coombe, England.

Another familiar hymn, "Glorious things of thee are spoken" (522/523, Hymnal 1982), written by John Newton (1725-1807), says that Zion, the City of God, is founded on the Rock of Ages.

Jesus might be appropriately symbolized by a rock out of which, once broken, poured the eternal waters of the Gospel, Holy Baptism and our salvation.

RAINBOW

A rainbow may be no more than an arc of prismatic colors in sequence caused to appear in the sky by the refraction, reflection and dispersion of sunlight in falling rain or mist. There is no pot of gold at its end, nor is one likely to find the Land of Oz by studying meteorology.

As a Christian symbol, the rainbow depicts the union between God and humankind (because its apex is in heaven while its ends touch the earth), and is a symbol of reconciliation (after the story of the Flood in Genesis).

In Renaissance art, the rainbow is sometimes employed as the throne of God. For example, some paintings of the Last Judgment show Christ seated on a rainbow. This imagery follows Revelation 4:2-3 in which the Lord's throne is described as surrounded by a rainbow.

A 9th century BC relief of the Assyrian god Ashur shows him drawing back the rainbow to launch an arrow. A similar use occurs twice in the Old Testament. There is a wordplay in Hebrew because the word "geshet" means both "bow" and "rainbow." Thus, in Lamentations 2:4 and Habakkuk 3:9-11 the writers depict the rainbow as a weapon for launching the Lord's wrath in the form of lightning and thunder.

Rainbows appear in several visions recorded in Holy Scripture. Ezekiel's vision of God compared the radiance surrounding God to that of a rainbow in the clouds

(1:28). St. John's vision of an angel descending from heaven through the clouds says that the angel had a rainbow wrapped around its head (Rev. 10:1).

The figure of the rainbow appears only twice in the Apocrypha, both times in Ecclesiasticus. Verse 43:11 calls it a bow bent by the hands of God and a cause to praise its Maker.

The most popular meaning of the rainbow is as a symbol of the everlasting promises of God. The Lord chose the rainbow as a sign of his assurance never again to destroy the world by a flood (Gen. 9:11-17). Christian interpretation of this symbol turns it around from a promise not to harm the earth to a promise of God's present upholding and nurture of his creation.

EAGLE

Most Americans think of the eagle primarily as a symbol of the United States of America. It was much earlier used as a symbol in the Hebrew Scriptures and culture, and in the New Testament and the early Church. At least five species of eagles are known to live in or migrate through modern Israel, which suggests that a variety of such birds was known there in biblical times.

The references to eagles in Psalm 103:5 and Isaiah 40:31 refer to a folk belief that an eagle renewed its strength by flying close to the sun and then plunging into water. In Exodus 19:4, God tells Moses that God "bore you on eagles' wings" out of the land of Egypt.

The references in Ezekiel 1:5, 10 and Revelation 4:7 describe four living creatures around the throne of God—man, lion, ox and eagle. Each of the symbols of the four living creatures in Revelation was interpreted by the early Church as one of the evangelists. The eagle was ascribed to St. John the Divine because he soared up to heaven in his contemplation of the nature of Jesus, thereby coming closer to God than any other person. The early Church also used a flying eagle as a symbol of Christ's Ascension.

Irenaeus compared the Holy Spirit to an eagle "hovering with his wings over the Church." Eagles appear on some early baptismal fonts, probably in connection with the legend reflected in Psalm 103. In some depictions of the Passion, an eagle made of silver or bronze is shown atop a standard. This was a Roman military symbol carried by the legions, although it is unlikely that such an eagle standard was present at the Crucifixion. In early Christian art, an eagle clutching a serpent in its talons or beak is a symbol of Christ's triumph over evil, Satan and death.

The modern Church derives its symbolic use of eagles from the Holy Scriptures and the early Church. Because the eagle is seen as a symbol of the inspiration of the Gospel, classic lecterns, which hold the large Bible from which the lessons are read, are sometimes shaped like an eagle with outstretched wings. Some parish churches dedicated to the Ascension place an eagle on their seal or banner.

The Hymnal 1982 contains no hymns which use the symbol of the eagle, but there is a popular religious song, written in 1979 by Michael Joncas, based on Psalm 91, the refrain of which begins "And he will raise you up on eagle's wings." This song might well be used at the Vigil of Pentecost or when Proper 6 is used in Year A, where it would amplify the reading from Exodus.

LANTERN _____

Both the Old and the New Testaments refer to lamps. From the excavation of ruins dating to biblical times, these lamps are known to have been simple containers for oil—usually olive oil—fitted with a wick or wicks, burned both to provide domestic illumination and for ritual purposes. Olive oil produces a smokeless flame and was thus especially useful for the interior lighting of homes.

The Romans developed a lantern which was very much like an oil lamp, except that it was fitted with sides of dried bladder or with plates of translucent horn, which permitted the light to escape but prevented the wind from extinguishing the flame.

The only mention of lanterns in the entire Bible—Old and New Testaments and Apocrypha—is in John 18:3. This verse describes a band of men carrying lanterns, torches and weapons, who were led by Judas to arrest Jesus. Because of this single reference, a lantern sometimes appears in art as a symbol of the betrayal of Christ.

The reference in Zephaniah 1:12a to God searching Jerusalem "with lamps" probably refers to lanterns, rather than to household lamps, because of their portability.

In addition to lanterns depicted in paintings and icons of the betrayal of Jesus, a lantern appears on the heraldic crest of St. Christopher along with a staff. These symbols are both reflective of the pious legend of St. Christopher carrying Jesus on his back across a river. The lantern suggests that, by carrying Christ, he bore the Light of the World.

In some churches, a tower is built over the transept or in the dome, into which numerous windows are fitted to permit the entry of natural light into the church. This tower is sometimes referred to as "the lantern," doubtless because, when seen from below, the view resembles the inside of an ancient Roman lantern.

The hymn, "O Christ, the Word Incarnate" (632, Hymnal 1982) refers to Holy Scripture as "a lantern to our footsteps."

SHIP/BOAT

A boat or ship served as a symbol for the Christian Church for people as early as the 4th century and quite probably earlier. The connection between the Church and a ship finds biblical warrant in the story of Noah and the ark (Genesis 6:13-8:19). Just as the ark protected Noah, his family and the animals, from the chaotic waters of the Flood, so the Church protects the Christian community during its difficult voyage through the dangerous waters of living in the world.

Early biblical scholarship was typological in nature, that is, the scholar searched the Old Testament for people, places, things, and events which pre-figured events in the life of Christ. By this method, Noah's ark was regarded as a "type" or pre-figuring of the Ship of Salvation—the Church. St. Ambrose (4th century) thus compared the Church to a ship and its mast to the cross of Christ.

A ship is used in this manner on the seals of several dioceses of the American Episcopal Church. Similarly a ship appears on the emblem of the World Council of Churches, a cross forming its mast.

That portion of the church building in which the laity sit or stand is traditionally known as the nave. Most authorities suggest that this term derives from the Latin word "navis" meaning "ship." Others suggest that it may be a corruption of a similar Greek word meaning "temple."

In keeping with the notion that the Church represents the Ship of Salvation, some churches are built to resemble an inverted ship which, when seen from the inside, exposes the ribs and timbers like those of the frame of an old sailing ship. The biblical reference to Jesus using a boat as a pulpit (Luke 5:1-11) provides sufficient warrant for some pulpits built to resemble the captain's bridge on a sailing ship.

A ship appears on the heraldic shield of St. Jude, apostle and martyr, because he is reputed to have traveled by ship to many ports as he spread the Gospel. Because St. Nicholas of Myra (the one on whom Santa Claus is based) is regarded as the patron saint of sailors, he is often depicted in art with either a boat or an anchor in the background. The ship on the shield of St. Anselm of Canterbury represents the English Church which he guided through the treacherous waters of the 12th century.

MUSTARD SEED

"Mustard" may refer to any of a number of annual plants of the genus Brassica or to the seeds of some of its species (typically B. nigra) which may be ground to make a tasty condiment. In biblical times, these species of mustard were used for their oil, the seeds ground into a paste, and as an herb for cooking.

In all three of the Synoptic Gospels, Jesus uses the mustard plant in a simile about faith (Matthew 13:31-32; Mark 4:30-32; Luke 13:18-19). Jesus compares the Kingdom of God to a mustard seed and to the plant which grows from it. In Matthew and Mark, Jesus describes mustard as the smallest of all seeds; in Luke, Jesus says nothing about the seed's size. In Matthew, Jesus says that mustard becomes a great shrub and then a tree. In Mark, he says it grows into the greatest of shrubs. In Luke, he says it grows until it becomes a tree. There is no parallel in the Gospel According to John but there is a parallel in the apocryphal Gospel according to Thomas, in which Jesus says that mustard seed is "smaller than all seeds" and that it produces a large branch without specifying tree branch or shrub branch.

The Gospels record another teaching by Jesus about faith and mustard seeds. In Matthew 17:20, Jesus teaches his Disciples that faith the size of a mustard seed can move mountains. In Luke 17:6, Jesus teaches his Disciples that faith the size of a mustard seed can move a mulberry tree from its place in the ground into the sea.

That mustard which is common to Palestine neither grows from the smallest of seeds nor grows into the largest of shrubs, much less into a tree. The seed is larger than that of a radish; the resultant shrub grows about ten feet tall. Biblical literalists have struggled to find some other mustard which grows from small seeds into trees—without success. These sayings are examples of hyperbole: intentional overstatement to make a point.

The description of the mustard plant as a tree may suggest an attempt to connect the teaching about the Kingdom of God with two passages in the Old Testament (Ezekiel 17:22-24 Daniel 4:10-27) in which the Kingdom of God is compared to a tree.

The import of Jesus' use of the simile of the mustard seed is in how something significant grows from something so small as to be insignificant. The Kingdom of God grows from tiny beginnings, and a tiny bit of faith can produce major results.

This conversion of the mustard seed into a symbol of faith and of the growth of the Kingdom of God is often represented in jewelry made from a glass drop containing a mustard seed, often from the Holy Land.

SEVEN

The number seven is used repeatedly in biblical writing as a symbol of perfection or completeness. The Genesis story of the creation of the world is the first such metaphor. Many others follow. Jacob bows seven times before Esau as a sign of his complete submission (Gen. 33:3). Noah takes seven pairs of ritually clean animals into the ark and the rains come seven days after the Lord's instructions (Gen. 6:2-4). The friends of Job come to comfort him and stay seven days and seven nights (Job 2:13). Seven priests carrying seven trumpets circle Jericho seven times in order that the walls may tumble down (Josh. 6). Naaman is cured of leprosy by washing seven times in the Jordan River (2 Kings 5:10-14). The miracle of Jesus' feeding of the multitude involves seven loaves of bread. The first deacons were seven in number—Stephen, Philip, Prochorus, Nicanor, Timon, Parmenas, and Nicolas (Acts 6:3).

The Book of Revelation is addressed to seven churches in Asia Minor—Ephesus, Smyrna, Pergamum, Thyatira, Sardis, Philadelphia, and Laodicea—and is full of things numbered seven: lampstands of gold, stars, torches, seals on a book, angels, horns, eyes, heads, thunders, plagues, golden bowls, hills and kings.

The Church early adopted this biblical penchant for the number seven. Seven Penitential Psalms have been used on the Fridays in Lent since Medieval times: 6, 32, 38, 51, 102, 130 and 143.

The sacraments are counted as seven: Holy Baptism, Holy Eucharist, Confirmation, Ordination, Holy Matrimony, Penance and Unction. There are Seven Deadly Sins—Pride, Covetousness, Lust, Envy, Gluttony, Anger, and Sloth—and Seven Cardinal Virtues—Faith, Hope, Charity, Justice, Prudence, Temperance, and Fortitude.

In sacred art, seven is commonly associated with the gifts of the Holy Spirit described in Isaiah 11:2—wisdom, understanding, counsel, fortitude, knowledge, fear of the Lord, and piety. These are often depicted as seven doves circling the letters "SS" (which stand for "Spiritus Sanctum"), or as seven tongues of fire (which are also associated with the day of Pentecost). This imagery recurs in the Hymnal 1982; the "sevenfold gifts" of the Holy Spirit appear in hymns 225, 226, 227, 500, 503 and 504.

While numerology had a minor place in ancient Hebrew forms of mysticism, the use of seven as a Christian symbol is not magical at all. It derives from the sense of completeness with which writers of the Old and New Testaments used it as a metaphor.

Index

D __

E __

F __

G __

R __

S __